A STITCH IN TIME

Una Stubbs

With Graham and Sylvana Nown

WARD LOCK LIMITED · LONDON

With love to my family and friends,
especially Graham and Sylvana.

Acknowledgments

With special thanks to Roald Dahl for the quotation from
Danny The Champion Of The World; Chapel Music; Linda McDevitt;
and David and Kay Canter and Daphne Swan, authors of
Cranks Recipe Book for permission to use their version of
Surrey Raised Pie.

Photographs by Tom Mannion
Line drawings by John Castle
Cartoons by David Mostyn

© Una Stubbs & Graham and Sylvana Nown 1985

First published in Great Britain in 1985
by Ward Lock Limited, 82 Gower Street,
London WC1E 6EQ, an Egmont Company.

Text set in Monophoto Bembo
by MS Filmsetting Limited, Frome, Somerset

Printed and bound in Italy by
Sagdos SpA

British Library Cataloguing in Publication Data
Stubbs, Una
A stitch in time.
1. Home economics
I. Title   II. Nown, Graham   III. Nown, Sylvana
640   TX145

ISBN 0-7063-6391-4

CONTENTS

Midwinter Manoeuvres

THE BEGINNING

IT USUALLY hits me just as I am getting out the baubles to decorate the family Christmas tree. Kneeling in a sea of greenery and silver, it seems only yesterday that I was doing exactly the same thing. A year is really quite long, I suppose, but it goes ever so quickly. Unwrapping the tiny glass globes, I gaze at them morosely, as into some doom-laden crystal ball, and think: well, I didn't lose weight; or I didn't master bread-making, or I didn't get better at the piano. I'm always going to learn a language, too, but never have. On reflection, several of the things I never get around to are vanity things, like tightening my thighs, but there are so many I *could* have done. By this time next year I could speak Russian ... if I put my mind to it. It's not that I really waste a year, rather that I could have jammed more into it, instead of looking at others and thinking: well, it's all right for them – they've got the time.

So I decided to do something. Nothing meaningful like sitting in hand-woven dresses discussing intellectual concepts. Simply something that took my fancy. It's strange, because lots of people seem to think I'm terribly well organized, cleverly fitting in work with family and hobbies. It sounds like a charmed life, but it isn't true. I've had all the miseries and the hard times too. And although generally I enjoy looking after the home, and find it relaxing, sometimes there just isn't enough time to do everything.

As Quentin Crisp says: 'Dust looks no different after one year than it does after two.' We should get on and do what we want to do. It may mean pushing things aside, but as long as there's food and clean, dry clothes, and no one is neglected, does it matter? When life is tremendously busy you have to work out your priorities – and stick to them.

Odd as it may seem, I happen to love ironing and starching, for instance. But who says you have to iron sheets, as long as they are clean? I always feel intimidated by people who can do everything, and know everything. Then I remember that everyone has their weak points, and there is room for improvement in us all.

This year, I thought, I'll do it all differently – the meals, the house, the children, the holiday – time for action. I was in my local art shop, thinking about some needlework, when I bumped into a woman I had done a commercial with, a very high-powered producer, a really sharp lady. She was with a friend, who looked as if she was a businesswoman, rummaging around searching for a Stanley knife. I spotted the knives, and pointed them out, and she said: 'We've got to dash, Una, sorry – we're late for our picture-framing class.' Everyone seemed to be doing it. So I diligently trotted down to the Town Hall to ask for a syllabus for local evening classes, and found it quite uplifting.

If I went for one evening a week to Fulham and South Kensington Institute, which is no different from hundreds of others around the country, I could learn to be a coastal skipper, practise lip-reading, converse in Urdu, or conduct a swing orchestra. This, I thought, is living.

Lists are important.
I make them all the
time now when I get
into a muddle, which
happens all too often.
There you are, I say,
you didn't put
everything down
in order of priority.
I got the idea from
a dear friend of mine,
Douggie Squires, who is
so well organized. I
tried it and it works.
Probably because to
make a list you have
to stop, sit down
and
think
it
all
out.

Children are more difficult to organize. Like all of us at times, they tend to have their own form of logic. But changing your approach to the family, I find, can be fun. I remember a friend of mine at work asking: 'How are the children?' I instinctively replied: 'Oh lovely!' because they were just going through the cherub period. She laughed and said: 'You wait!' I distinctly recall thinking smugly: no, not mine – I've put in so much work. And then wham! Adolescence.

Of all the different stages, there is always one more difficult than the others, and none of us are prepared for it. Everyone goes through the hair and funny clothes stage, which to me is totally unimportant, as long as they don't do anything too permanent, like tattooes. If I had a daughter I would hate her to grow up – and I'd feel so dated. Imagine longing to put on a strapless evening gown with 'Bike Boys' across each bosom. Otherwise, I can't see much to get excited about. It always amazes me to walk down Kensington High Street and see women with umbrellas and handbags up in town for the day to see the sights. They titter away at all the dyed hair, and invariably have a mauve perm or a blue rinse themselves. Remarkably, they have probably been doing it for years and no one has ever laughed. And what objection could dad possibly have when he does his hair by winding one strand round and round his head, and sticking it down with lacquer. The honestly-I'm-not-bald look, as Billy Connolly calls it. Frank Bough looks quite handsome since he got rid of his. No, I feel it's definitely better to have a son who looks funny at fourteen, not one who turns into a dreaded Medallion Man at forty.

The more I ruminated, the more I strengthened my resolve. All those milestones of the year – spring-cleaning, holiday packing, birthday parties and Christmas lunch – are they a penance or a pleasure? How different would they be if we organized them honestly, the way we really wanted to?

Perhaps it's all a question of self-training and sticking to your guns. When I was at school I was threatened with expulsion for giggling. I giggled so much that I was told if I didn't stop it would make me fat. As it turned out, I have earned quite a good living from giggling, because that was all I was ever asked to do in *Till Death Us Do Part*. Unlike my elder sister Claire, and my younger brother Paul, I wasn't very good at anything at school, but I liked dancing. My parents sent me to a school in Slough where we had lessons in the morning and danced all afternoon. The staff warned me that I would end up in the back row of a third-rate chorus, but I proved them wrong by going straight into the chorus at the Palladium. At 5 ft 3 in I wasn't nearly tall enough, but I stood on tip-toe at the audition. Life in the chorus-line is rather like being in the army. The discipline is very strict, and I hated it, but I loved the theatre. I learnt that all dancers have to be extremely disciplined and, though I resented it when I was young, I can now see how much it has stood me in good stead. Everything we do requires effort of some kind but, having made it, there is a lovely feeling of achievement ... with discipline and determination we could dump Christmas lunch, and invite everyone to get tipsy and help themselves instead! Why destroy yourself scrubbing the house each spring, acquiring that obligatory summer tan, or shedding winter weight by throwing yourself ungraciously round the floor of an aerobics class, when you can do it *your* way.

It may not suit everyone but, goodness, think about the peace of mind, how the home could be a haven and the children happy. Well, if not exactly happy, then mesmerized, thoroughly entertained or embarrassed!

*   *   *

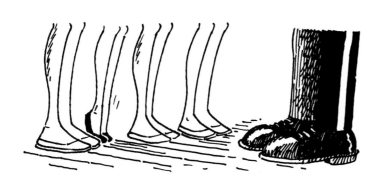

MIDWINTER MANOEUVRES

DECLARING WORLD WAR III on the house each year is one of those daunting operations at which other people seem to excel. I find it better to stagger the spring-cleaning rather than psyching myself up for one big blitz. Spring, in fact, is just about the worst time to spring-clean. My favourite time is around February, in those dreary weeks when it's nice to be indoors. Cupboards, drawers and wardrobes can be cleaned whatever the weather, and the bleak midwinter seems ideal to prepare for the bright, sunny days of spring. There is nothing quite like a good old clear-out to make you feel positive and saintly on the gloomiest of days.

I say to the children: 'Come on, we'll have a let's-be-ruthless day.' I get them to gather up the toys, books and clothes they have grown out of, or don't need any more, and we bundle them up for the Oxfam shop. If there are things you feel you can't afford to give away, you can always take them to those shops that sell them for you – though I had rather a chastening experience in one. I'd washed and pressed some clothes the children had grown out of, and neatly packed them into a suitcase. They had hardly been worn and were in very good condition, so I took the Tube and headed for Sloane Square, where I'd heard there was an ideal place to sell them. I walked into the shop and approached a lady who must have been at least a duchess – in attitude, if nothing else.

She picked through our things, with one finger and thumb, and said stonily: 'I'm afraid we can't *possibly* take any of these . . .' I stood there feeling such a twit. I suppose I should have realized that they took things only in absolutely pristine condition, with designer labels or at least some terribly up-market name. So I was left humbly to repack my case, like some unsuccessful travelling salesman, and trudge head-down back to the Tube station.

Midwinter manoeuvres

I find that a matching set of padded coathangers greatly improves the look of my wardrobe, and helps to keep the shape of my clothes. Although I had mine specially made, they really are quite easy to make yourself.

A Stitch in Time

When I get the worst of the housework out of the way in the winter, there is always a clean, refreshing feeling when spring comes round. I can actually enjoy going out without feeling guilty. Once the home has been cleaned through, and the cupboards and drawers are tidy, it's quite surprising how quickly you can rip through the day-to-day chores.

When I have a polishing spree I like to use wax polish on the furniture, or a bottle of white Min Cream. Polishing is a rewarding task, and certainly scares away floppy kimono arms. Most jobs are easier if your tools are looked after, and the humble duster is no exception. Even if it is only an old T-shirt, I make sure it is washed, dried and folded after use, and it works all the better next time. The only problem with dusty work is that I get cracked lips as I lick them in time with the polishing, so I have to apply a little lipsalve before I start. At Christmas, or when I haven't time to do any housework, I'm afraid it's just plumping up the cushions and dusting only the areas that catch the sun.

WARDROBE WARS

There is a certain age when we all become conscious of not wishing to look like mutton dressed as lamb. It does not mean that one can't dress stylishly, but the time has obviously come to avoid anything little-girly. A good way, I have found, is to think of a woman of similar type and build to myself, but perhaps a couple of years older, and imagine what she would look like in the outfit I have in mind. If she looks all right, then it's safe. There are several older women I admire, and by closely observing how they coped, I have tried to evolve my own style, adapting fashion to my age and size.

I firmly believe that if you are small, as I am, then *be* small – instead of striving to be medium-sized. Being small doesn't mean you can't wear the clothes and hats tall people can, simply that you have to scale them down accordingly.

The important thing is not to hang onto those clothes you hate yourself in, or that don't really suit you. I am ruthless about those endless outfits that never feel quite right, which I can't bring myself to get rid of. I give them to somebody else – and sometimes get a pleasant surprise in exchange. Trying to squash them all into the wardrobe simply makes a mess of the good clothes. It is a discipline which has hardly ever let me down. I've only once regretted parting with a skirt, a lovely black crêpe one that would have gone on forever. On the other hand, just one great sweater, or a pair of shoes you feel good in, always look nice if you look after them.

The first battle in the wardrobe war is to get rid of the naff coathangers, and all the wire ones. Make, or treat yourself to, a pretty matching set so everything hangs nicely. Padded hangers keep the shape of your clothes, and prolong their life. I had a great pile made up for me in a Provençal print at Soleado, in Fulham Road, and I hope to get some covered shoe-trees next. I swear by them – they are a real incentive to keep everything tidy and well looked-after. Covered hangers are quite easy to make yourself, and a print is a pleasant change from the usual satin-covered ones.

When all the boys have gone to bed, and I have a couple of hours to myself, I go up to my room, open the wardrobes and try to work out what goes with what. I have to do it, I suppose, because of my job though I must admit to some frightful mistakes.

Once on *Give Us A Clue* I tried to look really different and wore a silver skull-cap. But whenever the camera moved to a long shot it gave the impression that I was totally bald.

When the house is quiet I can work out whole outfits by putting a bit of this with a bit of that. There might still be life, say, in a pair of trousers if I put them with this sweater, or that blouse. It's nice to take stock of various ways you can use the same garment, with different tops, scarves or accessories, to make up a completely new look. Often, if you have to fly out of the house in the morning, things do not work out right when you try to match them together at the last minute.

It's surprising how much time and anguish you can save by going through the wardrobe and playing around with sweaters, blouses and accessories. I have to do it in complete secrecy because there's a lot of prancing about in front of the mirror, and face-pulling. You may not think you follow fashion, but your eye does. That floppy shirt you wear out with a belt and enormous beads was probably tucked in last year. The time I spend sorting out my wardrobe saves me hours, and when I'm shopping I usually know what I am looking for. Sometimes, if I see a bargain I know instantly if it will go with what I have at home. It's a method I've had to work out simply because I was so guilt-ridden by the many white elephants I've bought in the past.

I buy the best clothes that I can afford, because I find that it's more economical in the end. I bought classics before classics became fashionable, and I'm still wearing them six years later. Only now it's with opaque tights and flat shoes, rather than sling-backs and flesh tights. I take a basic outfit, and give it a start generally with navy blue or black, before adding fashion fads in jewellery, scarves, shoes and tights. Nowadays, it is open season with hemlines, and they are no longer a problem. Two years ago, for instance, I might have worn an outfit with flat boots, now I'll wear it with flat shoes and different accessories. It is just the same outfit, but the little touches make a world of difference.

Occasionally I splash out on shoes. I have one very expensive Chanel

A Stitch in Time

pair which I wear all the time, and receive lots of letters from viewers about. I originally bought them because they are marvellous for fat legs like mine. They are cream with a black toe-cap, and after six years they are still in beautiful condition. Whenever the heels begin to wear I get them repaired immediately. I keep a little box with a duster and some neutral polish handy to give my shoes a final rub before leaving home.

A friend of mine gave me a box full of silk flower sprays. At the time I thought: I'll never use those, but I'll keep them. And, sure enough, I use them now. I have a bright blue skirt, quite old-fashioned, which I wear with a long droopy black sweater because the bright blue isn't good next to my face. So I pick up the colour by putting one of the blue flowers by the neckline. I'm glad I've got things like that.

In late January, or February, after the Christmas rush, junk shops are often quite happy to haggle over small items. If you see some pretty beads reasonably priced, and you have nothing to go with them, splash out. In two or three years you can take them out, and perhaps complete an outfit because they make such an unusual colour combination. I love collecting bits and bobs, odd scraps of lace to fix around a neckline, and all those tiny things which can make or break an outfit, such as crystal beads, or a rather special brooch.

I keep my tights rolled up in a pretty basket, and beautifully-pressed satin ribbons rolled up in a box. I can't bear mangy powder puffs, but I like loose powder, so I now have a little pile of absolutely dazzling white ones. When one becomes grubby I throw it in the wash with the towels. To ensure they don't unravel in the washing-machine and burst open, I embroider round the edges in feather stitch.

Instead of a jumble of beads, which require patient untangling, I drape them on a hanger, usually with the clothes they particularly go well with. So every time I open my wardrobe to take something out, or put something in, it is always a pleasure and a joy. Everything is clean and pressed and looks neat and accessible. In my job it costs me time to squash and prod things into minute spaces. You can spend many a frustrating hour searching for a scarf which you feel sure is around somewhere. I can see at a glance what needs pressing and starching, or any little running repairs that may be needed.

I feel the same about the boys' clothes, too. I love it when they are wearing an absolutely squeaky-clean, eye-blindingly white T-shirt which maybe has a couple of darns. I use one of those little wooden darning mushrooms for all the family things, along with Chadwick's mending cotton. I also keep scraps of wool, though with the man-made element in clothes, there isn't half the need for it there used to be.

The dreaded man-mades have relegated darning to a dying art, but I love a neat little mend. When it is beautifully done I don't think it

detracts from clothes at all. A friend bought an old table-cloth which she took home and washed and starched. When she looked closely at it, she was amazed to find it covered in a multitude of tiny darns. They didn't in any way diminish its appearance and, if anything, made her even more proud of it.

Men are far worse than women when it comes to throwing out old clothes. There is always an old jacket they hang onto with affection, but look really dreadful in. If my eldest son hasn't worn something for a while, I hide it. When he says: 'Mum, have you thrown away that...?' I answer vaguely: 'No, it's around somewhere...' I have a secret drawer I hide them in until he forgets about them. It relieves me of the burden of doing the wrong thing – actually chucking them away.

THE LOST ART OF LAUNDERING

If you are thinking by now that you would love to give me a hearty kick in the shins for being so organized, please don't – because I'm not. I get myself organized only in spasms, because of a heavy work-load with television, or public appearances. The rest of the time I take short-cuts in so many ways. When I haven't time to bake or cook, then it's off to Marks & Sparks food department. So long as the ingredients are good, and no preservatives are added, we manage until it is convenient. And just because I enjoy washing and ironing doesn't mean I do it all every week.

In my old age I take a real pride in getting my whites really white. That old ad asking: 'Which mum uses Persil?' must have eventually got through to me. Nevertheless, some weeks the clothes may well go straight from the dryer into the drawers, neatly folded, of course! In winter, when I am pushed, I iron collars and cuffs, and down the front of shirts, because no one looks under jumpers. If you are desperately short of time, why get in a tizzy when you can fold neat piles of clean, dry clothes, or pull the sheets tight across the bed?

I suppose looking after clothes has always been second nature to me because, in my line of work, appearance is obviously important. And as I have been through the lean times, I have learnt how to make the best of what I have. No matter how rushed I am, I never put sweat-shirts, pullovers or silk in the tumble-dryer. For the best results I always wash by hand, though some would do equally well in the wool wash of the machine. Many pure new wool garments carry 'Dry-Clean Only' labels, but I have hand-washed them and been very pleased. On the other hand, I once washed a garment with a lining and the result was a disaster – I certainly wouldn't do that again! I try not to wring out tightly, but just squeeze them lightly and put them on a gentle spin. Wet wool easily pulls out of shape, so I arrange it carefully before hanging, or laying flat to dry. Silks often iron better slightly damp, so I roll them in a tea-towel until I'm ready to do them.

I remember the golden rule my mother taught me: never more than hand-hot for washing and rinsing. Treat your clothes like baby's skin: don't use too much soap, and be sure to rinse thoroughly.

I used to get fed up with my towels and coloureds fading and becoming generally dull, so I changed over to white and never regretted it. I started buying white tea-towels, bath towels, T-shirts, sheets and underwear. I now have so many that there is never a problem getting a wash-load together. White goes with everything, and I really don't think that egg dripping down a white dressing-gown looks any worse than egg dripping down a brown one.

When you are doing your wash, you can put aside any items you intend to starch – although some weeks, of course, there are none. As most of mine are white cottons, I generally put them all together for washing at a high temperature to preserve their whiteness. I don't bother to dry them, but immerse them in a starch solution straight from the spin-dryer. I make up a strong solution for collars, table-linen, and anything I want extra crisp. For bed-linen, frocks and shirts I use a more dilute mixture. Some people prefer to spin them out and iron while they are still damp, but I prefer to spin mine and leave them until they are rock-hard. Then I dampen them down and press them. It sounds rather topsy-turvy, I know, but it always produces good results. Incidentally, if my starch mixture goes lumpy, I just whisk it with a hand-whisk until it's completely smooth – a good technique for lumpy custard and batter, too!

I really am a starch fanatic, to the point of actually getting more of a kick out of starching our old casuals than our best things. Clothes which have been starched before pressing don't crease and crumple half so quickly, and I'm sure they actually look cleaner and last longer. To many people starching seems too much trouble but, with automatic washing-machines and spin-dryers, it only takes a few minutes extra.

For dark clothes which have white collars and cuffs, or fiddly trimmings, I use a spray starch that I make up myself. I got so fed up with those aerosols that either don't spray properly, or run out before I have finished and are chronically expensive. I make up the starch mixture as directed and pour it into one of those plastic squeeze sprays from the chemist.

It seems silly to spend ages choosing clothes, to blow everything for want of a little effort in looking after them. French women have the right idea. They don't all have *haute couture* clothes, but what they do have they really look after. You rarely find a French girl throwing on crumpled clothes. Regardless of what they cost, a little effort pays off.

17

THE IRON LADY

I have fond memories of my Granny ironing when I was a child. All the windows and doors would be open as she laboured away behind a cloud of pantomime steam. It is very frustrating – I never get that lovely *PSSST*! that I want. My own iron never gets quite hot enough to give that super hiss of long ago. Perhaps it was something to do with the heavy old flat irons they used to use. I despair over modern gadgets. Spray irons never work for me more than a couple of months before they spit black spots over everything. I use my own laundry spray now, made from an old Windowlene squirter. Although I am often offered gadgets, or urged by hi-tech friends to buy them, I try to resist as much as possible. I think it's because I become so annoyed when they break down. As a result, I tend to do lots of things the long way round, but I don't resent it at all. Domesticity can be very relaxing, and gives me the chance to listen to the radio at the same time.

One of my friends once asked: 'How do you iron your sheets?' And I told her: 'I fold them into fifty, first.' I don't mind cutting corners when I have to. Then, maybe the following week when I've not so much work on, I look forward to a blitz of washing, starching and pressing, and tackling the small pile of clothes I put to one side for mending. I love planning a day at home like that. It helps me relax, and keeps me fit. A pile of ironing and an afternoon play on Radio 4 can be heaven itself. Or there are those story tapes you can borrow from the library. A lady I know learnt to speak French while doing the ironing – the keener she became, the more washing she did.

THE WAY WE WERE

I have always been fascinated by Victorian household hints. So many of them are the very essence of common sense, while others are quite mind-boggling and amusing:

'*Washing, ready and effective mode of*: Dissolve 1 lb of soap in three quarts of boiling water, the night before washing. Beginning to wash, put the soap into the dolly tub, add eight tablespoons of turpentine and six of hartshorn. Pour upon the above eight gallons of boiling water. Begin with the fine clothes. Dolly each lot about five minutes in hot water in another dolly tub, and next in blue water before putting them in the boiler. The quicker the washing is done the better. As soon as one lot is taken out of the dolly tub, put another lot in while the others are being rinsed. A little pipe-clay dissolved in the water saves half the amount of soap.'

Spring is in the Air

A WOMAN FOR
ALL SEASONS

WHEN I WAS EIGHTEEN – and still giggling – I was a dancer in the *Follies Bergere*. It was a London version of the Paris show, very mild and quite tame by today's standards. We all tottered round in high-heeled silver sandals, decked out in spangles and masses of floating feathers. I thought it all terribly racy and daring because there were nudes in the show. They had to pose absolutely still to avoid offending public decency, and wore regulation-size nipple caps. I rose to the occasion by trying to make myself look at least twenty-five. I yearned to be a sophisticated, simmering *femme fatale*, desperately modelling myself on a strange combination of Elizabeth Taylor and Joan Collins.

I really loathed looking young for my age, and tried in vain to disguise it with masses of black around the eyes, intriguing arched eyebrows, and lots of red lipstick. Although I was actually quite pretty, I was convinced I was plain and felt a wreck beside my immaculately-groomed sister, Claire. I longed to be sexy and voluptuous, but a thirty-inch bust was a definite disadvantage. Boys always seemed to be more interested in my sister, or my friends, so I set out to be amusing instead.

I was really very lucky, but my anxieties were twanging too much to appreciate it at the time. I didn't suffer from teenage spots, and I have always had good skin, but I was too busy worrying about my flat chest. Years later, when I was pregnant, I briefly basked in the glow of having enormous bosoms, but all good things come to an end. Today, on the odd days when I do look a fraction younger than my years, it's because I've managed to keep my make-up as natural-looking as possible.

The ideal way to keep one's looks is to get plenty of sleep, avoid tension and take life as it comes. Unfortunately we can't always do what we want. Life is interconnected with friends and loved ones and – although we wouldn't have it any other way – we just can't help becoming involved. Make-up can be a wonderful asset against the wear and tear of daily life, but wrongly chosen and badly applied it can look far worse than none at all.

I have never been out of work, except by choice, and I have been very lucky because work has fitted in with the family too. When my three boys were small, I worked in the theatre, and later in films and TV, so I was able to take them with me in the school holidays. Work, however, means constantly keeping up appearances. Leaving the chorus for acting came about by accident, really. I auditioned for a dancing part in Cliff Richard's film *Summer Holiday*, but they gave me an acting role.

Later, completely out of the blue, I was offered a part in *Till Death Us Do Part*, as Alf Garnett's daughter, which ran for ten years on television. I played Aunt Sally in *Worzel Gummidge* for four years before *Give Us A Clue* came along, but as a dancer I did masses of television work, including miming to pop records on *Cool For Cats*. Little by little, as I went along, I learnt to make the best of my looks without using make-up as total camouflage.

I found that you really don't have to wear expensive make-up, because basically all the ingredients are the same. The important thing is to keep what you have, ready to use. There is nothing worse than a messy make-up bag, and they soon get that way if you don't keep a close check on them. Throw out all those blunt pencils you don't use, and sharpen the ones you do. Make sure the tops fit properly, and always have a sharpener handy for lip-liners and eye-liners.

I find baby oil an ideal make-up remover because it also works on water-proof mascara. As it is inexpensive I can afford to be lavish, and clean off thoroughly – every woman's most valuable make-up asset is a clean face and a clear complexion. When we are young our skin retains more moisture, and has a high rate of cellular renewal. But as the years go by the renewal process gradually slows down, the skin loses its elasticity and small facial marks and lines become more pronounced. The only way to retain softness and smoothness is to put back the moisture.

I apply a cream moisturizer after cleansing, both morning and evening, with gentle upward strokes to the neck and face. As one becomes older it is important to get rid of that microscopic layer of dead skin which gives the face a dried-up look. I brush-off as I wash with a little wooden Harris brush made from pure bristle, but I expect a soft nail-brush would do just as well. Even women who prefer to wear little or no make-up need to cleanse and moisturize to protect their skin from the weather. In winter, and on those windy spring days when dust blows everywhere, it is an essential daily task.

I keep a bottle of pure glycerine at my bedside to use on my hands at night. Only a drop is needed, rubbed in well, and it lasts for ever such a long time. Although it feels a little sticky, and is therefore best applied just before sleep, it is wonderfully softening. I suppose if you are planning to cut down on washing the sheets you could always wear gloves! Do not apply glycerine to your face – it encourages hair growth. When my young son once pointed out the merest whisp of a whisker, you have never seen anyone run up the road to the chemist so fast for the pot of wax. There is a lot to be said for encouraging children to tell you everything. I would sooner learn news like that from them than a stranger!

I prefer not to apply a heavy make-up base, and found it easy to get used to wearing something lighter for daytime. I also like to use a very fine powder, exactly the same colour as my own skin, to protect and even out my complexion. I use only a tiny amount of rouge, in cream or powder form, and it is important to match-up carefully. Unless you are a very young girl wearing fashion colours, try to obtain a shade the exact colour of your natural blush, otherwise it is all too easy to look like a rouged-up Music Hall star.

Rest is far better than foundation, but life is never perfect. I use foundation for television work and, like most women, use a little for evening wear – generally a light-textured cream base dusted evenly with powder. Although I need a little colour, I avoid anything that looks unnaturally dark on my skin, or too thick – I'd hate to look like a cracked vase.

At night the skin settles and changes, and any lines or imperfections are more noticeable. As you become older it is better to use a powder eye-shadow. Anything oily will be absorbed into the cracks and lines and show them up. The same, I find, applies to lipstick. Fence around the lips with a lip-liner, and apply the lipstick just a little short of the line. Then gently dab with a tissue and re-apply the lipstick, again stopping just short of the liner. This prevents a blurred edge where the lipstick runs into the minute lines around the mouth.

When you become tired of your hair colour, think twice before darkening it as this tends to have an ageing effect. If you fancy a change, go lighter – it is so much kinder to the complexion, which sallows slightly over the years. Careful use of a soft blusher also helps to counteract this. But, again, go for the colour nearest your natural blushing colour, and apply it sparingly and smoothly. At my age I would rather have a natural appearance than be mistaken for an old Gaiety Girl.

I have a tendency to buy economy-size bottles and pots of make-up, which are generally functional and ugly, so I make a practice of

Opposite *I tend to buy things for the bathroom in economy-size bottles and then transfer their contents into attractive glass bottles. The bottles bring an air of sophistication to the bathroom and help to make even the cheapest bubble bath look expensively inviting.*

collecting pretty containers to transfer the contents into. I do enjoy wearing mascara but, as I hate to have clotted eyelashes, I apply it in light coats and gradually build up. Although I cleanse my skin religiously each night, I will often unashamedly clean around my eyelashes and keep my mascara on for a couple of days. I wouldn't recommend it to anyone with allergies, or sensitive eyes, but it does look quite nice going to bed!

I adore perfume, and generally stick with my favourite, Aromatics Elixir by Clinique. I spray it everywhere, and I love it because it is oil-based and has a lasting effect. It also happens to be the only one I can actually smell on myself. Perfume is such a personal thing, and you really have to shop around to find exactly the right blend to suit your skin-type and personality. So many perfumes smell wonderful in the bottle, but are completely hopeless on different people.

Many English women do not use perfume properly, applying a little dab here and there, and maybe a spot on a handkerchief. After finding one which suits you, ladle it on. I use it liberally on my pulse points and find it gives me confidence. Michael Aspel often passed compliments on my perfume when we worked together on *Give Us A Clue*. Of course, if you get through perfume quickly, and can't afford more, the toilet-water versions are cheaper – and you can be more lavish with them. Or go without for a while until you can afford your next bottle. You may find you appreciate it and notice the smell more. Sadly, you can only be lavish with good perfume. The really cheap ones would have everyone on the bus throwing up – which isn't exactly the desired effect.

Many old-fashioned beauty recipes are absolutely unbeatable, and I thought you might like to try one or two I have picked up along the way. They have a habit of turning out differently for everybody who makes them, so don't throw out all your beauty preparations just yet! But it is enormous fun to put the time aside to potter around making something just for yourself, and the smells that float through the house when you recreate Victorian beauty preparations are beautiful.

Rose oil for massaging the face and throat

This is a simple recipe, not at all messy to make, and very effective. The main ingredient is 125 ml ($\frac{1}{4}$ pt) bottle of Sweet Almond Oil, which can be bought at most chemists. If the assistant looks blank, it is also often called Almond Oil BP, Expressed Almond Oil or, if you want to impress, Oleum Amygdale. Chemists use it as a base for preparations for chapped hands, ear-drops and all kinds of toiletries, so it is safe on sensitive skin.

Pour the oil, which is pale yellow and made from almond seeds, into a bowl or wide-necked jar, and drop in the petals from half a dozen red roses (a handy recipe for the aftermath of Valentine's Day). Cover the jar, or bowl, and allow the petals to soak in the oil for several days. Victorians used to say that deep-red roses were the best, possibly because they give the finished mixture a nicer colour. Squeeze the petals by pressing them between two small wooden spoons, until all the oil is extracted. The petals are thrown away and the oil bottled for gently massaging the face and throat. This was a favourite mixture used by Victorian ladies to ward off lines and wrinkles, and there must be something in it because rose water is still accepted as an effective skin toner.

Lavender oil

One of the disadvantages of perfume on those balmy summer days in the garden is that it often acts as a magnet for all kinds of irritating gnats and midges. Granny's answer was lavender oil, which smells quite light and beautiful and is very effective for keeping insects at bay. It is very easily made in a wide-necked jar, which must be completely dry. Cover the bottom with a layer of lavender flowers, and on top of them place a thin pad of cotton wool soaked in olive oil.

Next sprinkle another generous layer of lavender flowers, followed by another cotton wool pad soaked in oil, until the 'sandwich' completely fills the jar. Screw on the lid or, better still, put a piece of glass on top, and place in a sunny window. After a week or two, squeeze the scented oil out of the cotton wool, and bottle it.

An extra joy, of course, is collecting the prettiest bottles, bowls and jars you can find to contain the oil and petals. And you can add to your collection on holiday when strolling round antique shops and flea-markets.

The beautifying bath

In the late nineteenth century, women were fond of using a muslin bag filled with oatmeal to cleanse the face, and I once found this wonderful recipe for 'a beautifying bath', tucked away between the pages of a

Victorian book. There were, in fact, several versions of the 'beautifying bath', which were said to keep the skin soft and pale. This was the most popular method. Put two large cupfuls of marjoram and mint, along with a teacup of fine oatmeal, into a muslin bag. Tie the top firmly and drop it into 3.75 litres (1 gal) of hot water to soak for half an hour. Then squeeze out the bag firmly, and add the water to your bath. I haven't tried it consistently enough to swear by its claims, but it smells beautiful and is very refreshing.

Another 'beautifying bath' can be made in the same way, using a generous handful of lavender flowers mixed with a similar amount of fine oatmeal, and the smallest pinch of powdered orris root. Orris can be bought from the chemist, and is used as a base for violet perfume. Many years ago there was a popular dusting powder, known as Violet Powder, which contained orris. People with hypersensitive skin, however, may be allergic to orris. The amount used in a bath sachet is hardly likely to produce a reaction, but if you are in any doubt make a test dab on your wrist. The finished bath mixture, made in the same way as the oatmeal sachet, has a subtle, flowery perfume, and is very relaxing.

Muslin bath sachets have a limited life because, once wet, the oatmeal does not last long. To economize, you can wrap the lavender in a smaller bag, and put it inside the bag containing the oatmeal, so that it can be used again. These homely bags can be tied with ribbon to make pretty gifts, especially with a hand-written, decorated card giving instructions and ingredients (unless you want to keep them a secret).

Similar bath-bags for men can be made in exactly the same way using freshly-dried, crushed pine needles, young pine shoots or any spicey-smelling herbs. They look attractive tied with dark-coloured cord, instead of a ribbon bow, and placed inside a gift box.

Mob-cap bags are simplicity itself to make. All you need is a circle of fine muslin, about 30 cm (12 in) in diameter, and edged with lace or

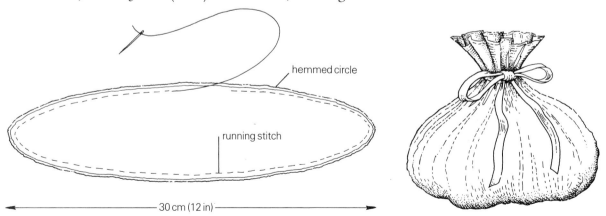

hemmed circle

running stitch

30 cm (12 in)

hemmed. If it is to be used over and over, the linen must have a firm, neat hem to stop it fraying

Make a row of running stitches about 4 cm (1½ in) from the outer edge, and lay the muslin flat to fill. When there is enough mixture in the circle, draw up the running stitch to make a pouch. Wind the cotton around a couple of times, finish off with a few neat stitches, and add a little ribbon bow for a pretty effect.

THE WAY WE WERE

'*To improve the complexion*: It is good to rise early in the morning, drink a cup of milk, walk into the fields, wash the face in sparkling dew, gaze on creation, below, above, and all around you, till mental pleasure beams forth on your face in radiant smiles.'

'*The Douche Bath*: Very efficacious in extracting the morbid humours from all the parts they have seized upon for years. It removes the weakness of the skin and strengthens it. It renders the body hardy, and fortifies it to endure all the changes of the air. It powerfully excites the muscular and nervous systems. The Douche Bath is a stream of falling water as thick as the wrist, and permitted to fall on the body from 12 to 18 feet.'

'*The sitz*: is a small shallow tub 18 inches in diameter, with water 3 or 4 inches deep, in which the patient sits, with his feet on the ground, for 15 minutes or more, twice or thrice per day. It wonderfully strengthens the nerves, draws down humours from the head and chest, relieves flatulency, a most important result to those who lead a sedentary life.'

DIARY CLOTH

SO MANY PEOPLE wrote to me after my last book, *In Stitches*, to say how they loved the idea of an autographed table-cloth. It strengthened my resolve to work on more traditional needlework items, which not only are of great interest, but they also become heirlooms, each telling a story about life as we have lived it.

I always date and sign my needlework, and it occurred to me as I was finishing off a cushion recently that I could start a cloth based on the year's events – a personal diary in linen. Not so much the great happenings of world-shattering importance; just the ones which affect me and those around me. As it was quite early in the year, I thought I would fill it in piece by piece, just like a diary. I thought about the size some time, and eventually settled for a coarse white linen cloth about 69 cm (27 in) square.

I worked the hem in ladder hemstitch, and added a smaller square within it. In the centre I embroidered a lovely swirly design which fitted well inside the drawn threadwork. As I worked I began collecting in my head a list of things that had happened, and wondered how to translate them into fabric and thread. At this stage I was trying the cloth on various surfaces – a trolley; placed across the centre of my big table in a diamond shape; then over a full-length cloth on a small round table. I found the size I had chosen easy to work with, and adaptable to all those various items of furniture. By trying it out first, I was able to decide on how to arrange the writing and pictures.

I finally made up my mind to place them at random, which seemed quite fitting – most years, after all, are something of a jumble and cluttered with happenings. It also proved less daunting – I didn't want a big gap for one month which may have been uneventful, and a very crowded month next to it.

A Stitch in Time

I hoped that by the end of the year it would be evenly crammed with little notes and pictures, the more higgledy-piggledy the better. When you begin, the cloth looks frighteningly blank, rather like starting a novel on a clean piece of paper. But it's surprising how quickly it begins to fill up. It is best, I think, to choose a stitch for the writing which you feel most comfortable with. If you find that using the simplest stitches makes it a pleasure to pick up the cloth and work on, then why not use them? I used split stitch for the writing because it is not too heavy, and I'm at ease with it. As a result, I whizzed along quite quickly and it never became a chore.

MAKING A START

Measure a 10 cm (4 in) margin on all four sides of the cloth, and mark out an inner square, in pencil if you wish, to use as a guideline for the drawn threadwork. Draw your first thread by using the tip of your needle to pull it gently from the middle of the line and snip it. Now draw the thread out to the edge and stop at the pencil line. Thread it into your needle and darn it into the edge of the fabric; repeat on the other side. Continue to draw five more threads, working towards the centre, and then draw six threads on the other three sides.

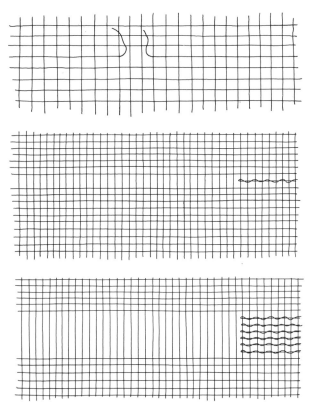

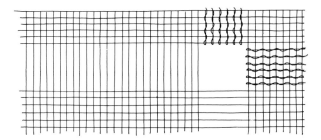

When you have drawn the threads along all four sides, turn in the edge and fold the hem so that it just meets the outer row of drawn threads. The corners will need trimming off, leaving just a tiny amount for turning in and sewing down.

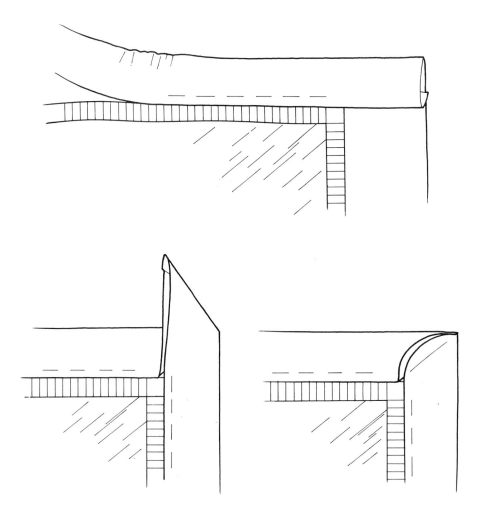

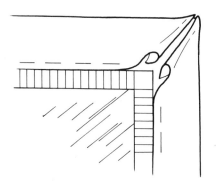
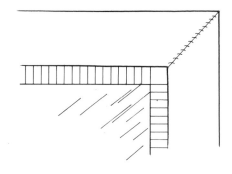

Ladder hemstitch

Working from right to left, bring the working thread out about two threads down from the drawn threads, through the folded hem, at the right-hand side. Pass the needle behind four loose vertical threads, then insert the needle behind the same four threads and through the hem in readiness for the next stitch.

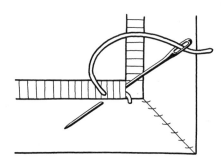
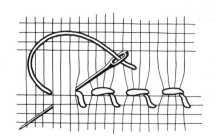

When all four sides are hemmed, repeat the stitch on the inside edge of the drawn threads, catching up only the single fabric instead of the folded hem.

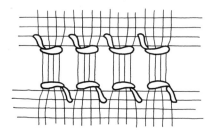

When you have worked ladder hemstitch on all four sides of the cloth the hemming is complete, so remove any tacking stitches.

A Stitch in Time

Central square

I worked another, smaller, square of ladder hemstitch (without the actual hem, of course) in the centre of my cloth to frame an embroidery design. It is best to work this about 2.5 cm (1 in) larger than your design.

You will find that making up your own design for the central square and planning the stitchwork is really absorbing, but it's also a pleasure to have an afternoon out selecting a suitable transfer and silks.

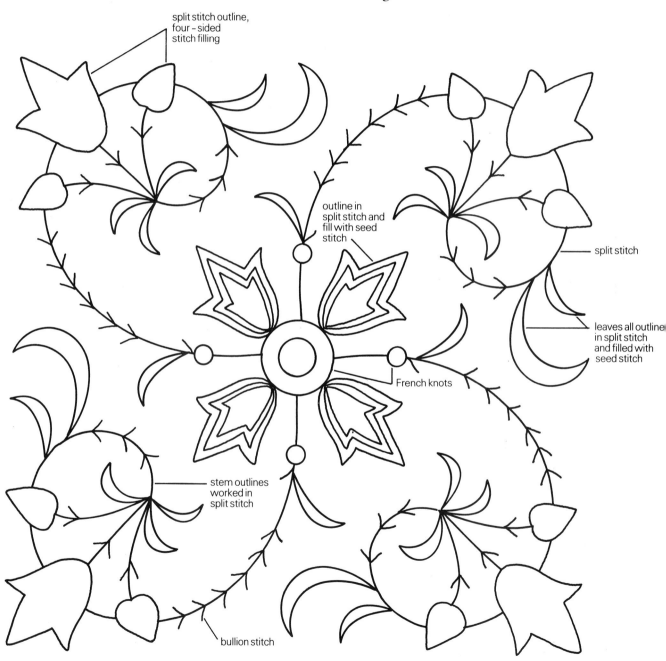

split stitch outline, four-sided stitch filling

outline in split stitch and fill with seed stitch

split stitch

leaves all outline in split stitch and filled with seed stitch

French knots

stem outlines worked in split stitch

bullion stitch

Unfortunately, I had to unpick some of my satin stitching as it appeared too heavy on the loosely-woven linen I had chosen. Finally, I did all the outlines in split stitch and filled in with four-sided stitch and seed stitch. I've discovered that some of the simplest little stitches are the most effective for fillings on a loose weave.

I have compiled a small selection of simple but very useful embroidery stitches at the end of this chapter.

Diary notes
Next I filled in the cloth with lots of happenings.

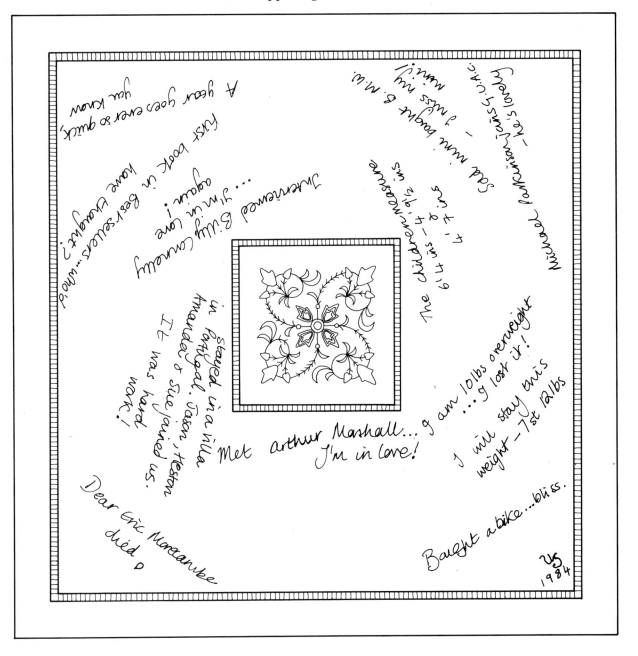

Stitches suitable for lettering and outlines

Backstitch

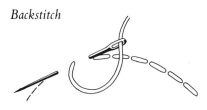

Chain stitch

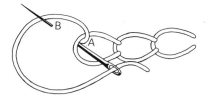

Needle and thread emerge at point A. Lay the thread in a small loop and hold it with your left thumb. Re-insert the needle at A and bring it out again a little ahead, at B. Be sure the needle comes up through the loop as you draw the thread through. Continue the chain, inserting the needle exactly where the thread last emerged.

Split stitch

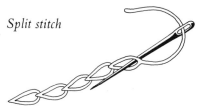

Working left to right, make a small straight stitch along the design line. Then take a smaller backward stitch on the reverse which splits the top stitch as it emerges. Draw the thread through and repeat. Keep the stitching regular to produce a fine, flat finish.

Stem stitch

Work from left to right, taking regular, slightly slanting stitches along the line of the design. The thread always emerges on the left side of the previous stitch. This stitch is used for flower stems, outlines, and so on. It can also be used as a filling: work rows closely together within a shape.

Simple filling stitches

Backstitch trellis

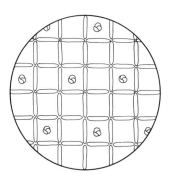

This is a simple backstitch worked in a trellis pattern with occasional French knots dotted in here and there.
It is best to work your parallel lines of backstitch in rows, and then cross them at right angles with another set of parallel rows. You can work your trellis straight, in squares, or on the diagonal.

French knot

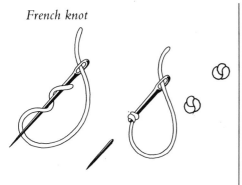

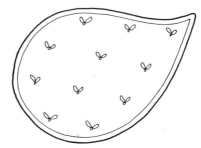

The thread comes through at A
and the needle is inserted at B.
Pull the thread through gently,
then bring the needle through
at C to tie down the loop,
forming a 'V' shape.

Cross stitch filling

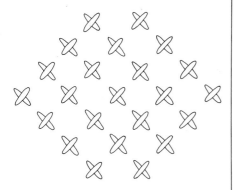

Seed filling stitch

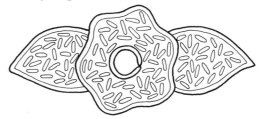

Tiny stitches all of even length
placed randomly and at
different angles.

The cross stitches can be
worked in rows all touching
each other, or they can be
spaced.

Detached fly stitch

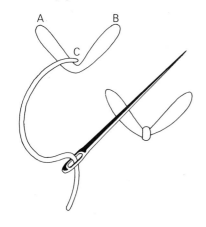

Detached chain stitch

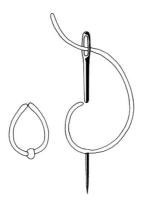

Another simple little filling that gives a 'powdered' effect.

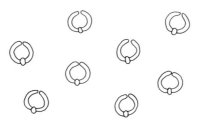

Four-sided stitch

This stitch is worked from right to left and can be used as a border or a filling. Bring the thread through at the arrow; insert the needle at A (four threads up), bring it out again at B (four threads down and four to the left).

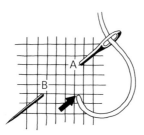

Insert at the arrow, bring out at C (four threads up and four threads to the left of A).

Insert again at A and bring out at B. Continue in this way to the end of the row or close the end for a single four-sided stitch.

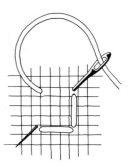

To use as a filling stitch

Turn the fabric round for next and all following rows and work in the same way. Pull all stitches firmly.

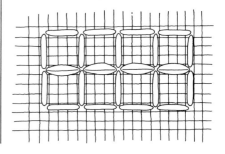

Some much used and favourite embroidery stitches

Bullion stitch

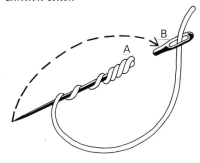

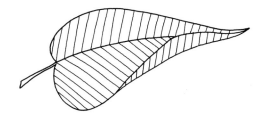

Bring the thread through at A and insert needle at B. Allow the point only to emerge at A again. Twist the thread around the needle point until it resembles a cord long enough to cover the space between A and B. Hold the twists with your thumb and carefully draw the needle and thread through, until the coil lies flat in the correct position between A and B. Take the thread to the reverse, inserting at B and either make a second stitch or fasten off.

If your design is drawn in sections, fill in one section at a time. By slanting the stitching at different angles for each section you can give the finished work shade and texture.

Straight stitch

Sometimes called single satin stitch, this stitch is used only to cover small straight lines. The stitches are placed singly and may vary in length and direction.

Satin stitch

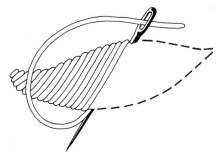

Taking care to form a neat edge, straight stitches are closely worked to cover a design shape.

Summer Days

A GARDEN OF DELIGHTS

I LOVE FLOWERS. Nothing finishes off a cleaning day better than arranging masses of them around the house, they give me such a tremendous lift. It can of course prove expensive if, like me, you live in town. When flowers are scarce, for one reason or another, I fill out the vases with leaves or budding twigs. Chatting-up neighbours whose garden blossoms hang over onto the pavement can be fruitful too, and I have often taken advantage of their generosity.

In summer I love an abundance of flowers in the house, along with a huge bowl of polished apples. One of the nicest things about the warm months is the chance to collect fallen flower heads, petals and leaves with the children. Pressing them between tissue in books is a great family delight. When the weather gets colder, younger children love to spend an evening or wet afternoon making them into thank-you cards, or gift tags. Aunts and grannies particularly appreciate something the children have made themselves.

In autumn, bowls of gleaming conkers look beautiful in the house – and by encouraging the boys to contribute to the family collection on the kitchen table I avoid the gruesome discovery, several months later, of strings of green mouldy conkers in the bottom of their wardrobes! Conkers and a bowl of dried copper leaves bring a lovely breath of autumn into the house.

At Christmas I like to do the same with fir cones, fir twigs and holly, which give the kitchen a fresh, outdoor smell.

My own town garden is very small – pocket-size, really – and I find great joy in filling it with those flowers which make cottage gardens so beautifully hazy. At times it grows into a glorious wilderness. Each year I solemnly promise myself that I will be a better gardener, but other priorities always seem to pop up. I do, however, like it to be pretty, but

Opposite Why not make a batch of your own potpourri to provide a hint of summer indoors all year round. I have a large basketful, decorated around the brim with dried flowers, which stands in a kitchen corner. I find an occasional shake of the dried petals fills the air with a beautifully fragrant smell.

I have to be careful what I plant because of the fumes from London traffic. Geraniums, daisies and ivy have so far proved the hardiest, but next year I plan to cram it with white marguerites.

I am always hunting for attractive vases and plant containers. Even the humblest chipped jug is as great a thrill to find as an expensive piece of crystal. I have as much affection for one of these on my kitchen dresser as the most expensive vase in my sitting room. It is important to keep vases clean, not only because glass magnifies even the smallest specks of dirt, but because bacteria lurking in dirty vases shortens the life of your flowers. You can have several days more joy from them by spending just a few minutes scrubbing inside a stained vase with an old toothbrush. If the marks are very stubborn, an hour soaking them in a weak solution of bleach and water saves elbow grease, but the container must be thoroughly rinsed afterwards.

I also tackle discoloured vases or decanters by stirring 25 g (1 oz) of salt and a large spoonful of vinegar into warm water. If you shake it around the container and leave it to stand for an hour or two, before rinsing with soda water, it works a treat. To obtain a nice final gleam on my crystal vases I rinse them in a solution of vinegar and water, and polish them with a linen cloth.

Everyone has their own favourite method of extending the life of cut flowers, though some seem to work better than others. A little pure glycerine in the water, for instance, is very effective with gypsophila, or Baby's Breath, one of my favourite flowers. A florist told me that lemonade, or even water to which a little sugar has been added, will revive most flagging flowers. With spring varieties, however, nothing equals a pinch of salt. Another good remedy for blooms which are beginning to droop is to put the bottom third of the stalk into hot water and leave it there until the water becomes cold. Then cut off the end of the stalk and put the flower into a vase of water in which a little saltpetre has been dissolved. The reviving effect is quite amazing. Whenever I have to go away I keep pot plants moist by standing them on a well-soaked old towel in the kitchen sink.

ELIZABETHAN AIR FRESHENERS

There is a lady in Nottingham, Domini Gregory, who enjoys nothing better than a nice thick ham and rose petal sandwich when she feels peckish. Mrs Gregory, who is fortunately married to a rose-grower, has also converted her three children to rose petals and salad, and rose petal sponge cake too. She simply washes them, dabs them dry and removes the bitter-tasting eye at the base of the petal before serving. It is nothing new: eighteenth-century soldiers at the Battle of Minden, in north Germany, munched rose petals from the fields to sustain themselves.

Most of us, however, find the perfume rather than the taste, appealing. The Elizabethans were among the first to discover that the delights of potpourri last for several years. There were many devoted enthusiasts among the aristocracy. Sir Hugh Platt wrote a little book of instruction in 1594, called *Delights For Ladies*, in which he claimed that his own potpourri would perfume his linen for seven years. Recipes were adjusted for particular purposes, such as removing musty smells from furniture, or stuffing pillows to cure insomnia. I have a large basket, decorated around the brim with dried flowers and filled with potpourri. It stands, unashamedly twee and nostalgic, in a little kitchen nook where I keep all manner of shopping baskets and wicker trays. Just an occasional shake of the dried petals is enough to pervade the air with a beautifully fragrant smell.

Potpourri has hardly changed at all over the centuries. While the world around us hisses with aerosols, it remains a collection of dried flower petals and leaves, mixed with powders and spices – the original Elizabethan air freshener. There is little to beat the sheer enjoyment of a family project to make your own from home-grown flowers. When the petals are brittle after drying, you can blend your own fragrance by trial and error by adding finely-chopped or grated dried orange and lemon peel, a few cloves, pieces of crumbled cinnamon stick, rough salt and powdered orris root. Even if you only have a window box, it is fun to make a small amount of your own potpourri to provide a hint of summer indoors all year round. Alternatively, you could buy a potpourri base and add extra flowers and fragrances to it.

The secret is to pick a sunny day. Collect flowers straight from the garden – those that have been cut for some time are not effective. It is best to pick young flowers and leaves as they are beginning to open. Gather them in the old way, when the morning dew has dried, remembering that potpourri tradition says that flowers growing in warm, sunny spots give the finest perfume. Correctly made, your potpourri should last for years, with only an occasional pinch of salt and perhaps a few drops of lavender water or rose water to revive the fragrance.

A good potpourri should be a mixture of heavily-scented flowers, such as roses, geranium leaves, lavender, rosemary, violet, carnation, thyme and whatever else takes your fancy. Do collect tight buds, too, and to make it more attractive throw in flowers which, though not strongly fragrant, add a splash of colour – cornflowers, marigolds, and pansies, for instance.

When all is safely gathered in, lay your harvest out one by one – only small, tight rosebuds need not be separated – on tissue or absorbent paper. Some people like to dry their flowers out in the sunshine, but if

I am always hunting
for attractive plant
containers – baskets,
bowls, jugs and vases of
all sorts – which I love to
fill with an abundance of
flowers. When flowers are
scarce I fill the vases with
leaves or budding twigs,
to bring a touch of the
country to my house
throughout the year.

the weather looks at all doubtful, a large window-ledge will do equally well. After a couple of days turn them all over, one by one, and leave them for another forty-eight hours. When they are absolutely dry, tip enough petals to fill a 1 litre (2 pt) container into an earthenware bowl and mix in 15 g (½ oz) of powdered orris root, which acts as a fixative, and 2 tablespoons of rough sea salt as preservative.

If you wish to give your potpourri a head-start, add a little lavender or rose water. Stir the mixture every day with a wooden spoon or skewer, and within a fortnight it should have matured enough to transfer to the bowl or basket you have chosen. Any left-overs can be stored for years in a dry, airtight container.

You might like to borrow some ideas from this original Elizabethan potpourri recipe: twenty-four fully-blown roses; six stems each of thyme, rosemary, sweet majoram, lavender, myrtle, balm, and sweet basil; two bay leaves; 'a little mint of all kinds'; one onion skin. When dry, crush into coarse powder and add 15 g (½ oz) of powdered cloves, musk, orris and cinnamon. Mix all the ingredients well.

A SUMMER HERB CUSHION

Even if your garden has failed miserably, you can make the most of it by basking through those balmy summer days on an old-fashioned herb cushion. Victorians loved them because they smelled so pleasant and, being practical people, they also liked them because they have a reputation for keeping flies at bay. And, of course, they give the house a beautiful reminder of summer right through the winter.

The cushion is filled with a potpourri mixture of dried lavender, rosemary, tansy, woodruff, southernwood, plus any sweet-smelling mixture of herbs you can put your hands on. As I have only a small garden it was easier to buy most of them from a specialist herb shop, already dried and prepared. The tansy, incidentally, is a fly-repellent – it also works a treat tied in little bundles and hung in the kitchen in summertime. If you are lucky enough to cultivate your own herb patch, dry your collection until it is quite brittle and rub it to a rough powder between your hands or two wooden spoons.

It is wise to make your cushion from finely-woven cotton. With a loose-weave fabric you run the risk of a herbal bottom every time you sit down. The outer case can be made from almost any material, depending on what purpose you have in mind. If you plan to keep the herb cushion in the bedroom, for instance, a delicate cover would be lovely. For the garden a strong linen or calico is more appropriate – especially if you have children who tend to kick them around in the pigeon-poo. To get the fullest fragrance from the filling, an inset of cotton lace, or any fine fabric, can be incorporated into your design. The inner bag can be taken out of the stout linen cover at the end of the summer, and slipped into a prettier one for your bed in winter.

CRACKPOT MOSAICS

There is always room for a folly in your garden, no matter how small! In centuries gone by, they were fond of building huge follies in the shape of Greek temples, towers which looked like pineapples, and even façades of entire houses, all of which served no useful purpose other than to decorate and amuse. I have a tiny folly in the corner of my garden, covered in pieces of broken china stuck on with cement. It is a hotch-potch of household pottery – all the pieces I have broken over the years but which, like a magpie, I couldn't bear to part with. It also counteracts the distress caused by breaking something that has sentimental value, and which cannot be repaired.

When I sit out on a summer's day, I can see bits of the children's old crockery, a long-serving teapot which I accidentally dropped, ornaments I still have great affection for, even fragments of broken mirrors. I wish now that I had also kept one of the Melamine pusher-spoons the children learned to feed themselves with. The idea of these sentimental little shrines began in France, where the best belongs to Raymon Edouard Isidore, a retired road-sweeper who has been described as one of the great naive artists of the century. His beautiful house near Chartres is absolutely covered – walls, floors and ceilings – with marvellous crackpot mosaics made from china found on rubbish dumps. My own modest effort is still growing, though it looks depressingly new. I have tried everything I can think of to encourage it to acquire a nice green mossy mould – from painting on old yoghurt, to brushing it with horse manure! – but it refuses to be hurried.

I am still collecting broken crockery. My next mosaic will replace one of the patio tiles in my yard, and will consist of crocks set into cement.

Now I never get upset when I break something of sentimental value which cannot be repaired. I simply collect the broken crockery in a large drawer for my next mosaic, which will replace one of the patio tiles in my yard.

Opposite and left
My very own garden folly, covered in pieces of broken china set into cement, has become a sort of sentimental shrine. It is a crackpot mosaic of all the pieces of household pottery I have broken over the years, and which I couldn't bear to part with, from the children's old crockery to beloved vases.

47

BEAUTY WITH A BITE

As much as I adore plants in the house, there are a handful which, no matter how beautiful, we should really think twice about if there are children around. They look the most innocent flowers imaginable, but it takes really only a moment when mum's back is turned for a toddler to break off a stem or pop a berry into his mouth. Plants should obviously be well out of baby's reach, but children can be at risk just from handling some varieties.

Among the common plants to beware of in your local florist's are *hyacinths*. While it is unlikely that even the most determined child would unearth the poisonous bulb and eat it, many people are allergic to the sap which is exposed when a leaf or flower is broken. *Winter cherry*, easily recognized by its orange berries, which appeal to children, is mildly poisonous, and can cause untold tummy problems if the tiniest part is accidentally swallowed. *Oleander*, which now seems to be on sale everywhere, has beautiful Mediterranean flowers, but a sap which is among the most toxic of all plants. Every part of the oleander is highly poisonous, causing severe abdominal pains and vomiting, and the seeds are fatal if eaten. *Leopard lily*, or *Diffenbadia*, also has a highly poisonous sap. It is easily recognized because of its large, spotty leaves. *Poison primrose*, on the other hand, is not really poisonous at all, but if handled the leaves can cause rashes and skin irritation. *Poinsettia*, those popular pot plants with large red flowers, has sap which causes skin blisters, and the leaves can induce bowel pains and delirium if eaten. It all sounds rather alarmist, but if children are around it is wise to think carefully when planning to beautify the house. Pot plants are often an impulse buy, but in inquisitive little fingers can be quite worrying.

THE WAY WE WERE

'Gather a wreath from the garden bowers,
And tell the wish of thy heart in flowers.'

The Language of Flowers

Flower	Sentiment
Alyssum (sweet)	*Worth beyond beauty*
Bluebell	*Constancy or sorrowful regret*
Broom	*Humility, neatness*
Buttercup	*Ingratitude*
Camellia Japonica, white	*Perfected loveliness*
Carnation Red	*Alas! for my poor heart*
Striped	*Refusal*
Yellow	*Disdain*

Clematis	*Mental beauty*
Crocus (spring)	*Youthful gladness*
Daffodil	*Regard*
Dahlia	*Instability*
Daisy	*Innocence*
Elder	*Compassion*
Everlasting Pea	*Lasting Pleasure*
Fern	*Sincerity*
Foxglove	*Insincerity*
Geranium	*Sorrowful, melancholy spirit*
Hawthorne	*Hope*
Hollyhock	*Fruitfulness*
Honeysuckle	*Bonds of love*
Ivy	*Friendship*
Lady's Slipper	*Fickleness*
Larkspur	*Levity, lightness*
Lilac	*First emotion of love*
Lilac (white)	*Youth*
London Pride	*Frivolity*
Marigold	*Inquietude*
Mimosa	*Courtesy*
Narcissus	*False, delusive hope*
Oak	*Hospitality*
Orange Blossom	*Your purity equals your loveliness*
Pansey or Heartsease	*Think of me*
Periwinkle	*Sweet remembrance*
Pink	*Lively and pure affection*
Rhododendron	*Danger*
Rose	*Beauty*
Rose White	*Silence*
Rosebud White	*The heart that knows not love*
Snap Dragon	*Presumption*
Snowdrop	*Hope*
Strawberry	*Perfect excellence*
Sweet Pea	*Delicate pleasures*
Tuber-rose	*Voluptuousness*
Tulip Red	*Declaration of love*
Variegated	*Beautiful eyes*
Yellow	*Hopeless love*
Violet Blue	*Faithfulness*
Yellow	*Rural happiness*
Virginia Creeper	*I cling to you both in sunshine and in shade*
Zinnia	*Thoughts of absent friends*

GLORIOUS FOOD

IF THERE COULD be only one heavenly memory of childhood, for me it would be coming home and opening the door to the mouth-watering smell of home-baked food. It instantly signalled that mum was home, and all was well in my cosy little world. Today, especially if you are a working mother, baking is a nice thought but there is often so little time to put it into action. From time to time, if you have a day off work, it can be relaxing and rewarding to try a whole new family menu. On those really dreary winter days I'll do a whole mound of baking, which makes the house smell wonderful. Just before the children are due home I light lots of ordinary household candles and plant them everywhere. When they walk in, it is lovely to see their faces. It is particularly heart-warming if you have central-heating, and your children are not used to the glow of an open fire. They love the snugness and smell and novelty of it all. Well, they loved it when they were younger; now they think it's a bit soppy. I find it a very satisfying way of making something special of an ordinary weekday away from work.

I simply fail to understand why the Great British Sunday Lunch has to be made on a Sunday – the only day of the week which most of us have completely free. In years gone by, it was the only time the family were able to sit down together for a 'proper meal'. That, of course, does not apply so much now – food has changed, and it is far more practical to have Sunday lunch, say, on a Monday. With more women working than ever, Sunday has become perhaps the only day when all the family can go out together. We enjoy a simple, filling lunch, but I have made a point of cutting out all that mother-fussing-in-the-kitchen-all-day-Sunday ritual. I made the decision to devote the day to my family, if they want to be with me, or sometimes even to myself. When we do go to the park, the whole place is empty until four o'clock because everyone is still at home finishing off the pots. When they finally arrive, the place is full of harassed, over-full, over-tired mums trying to keep up with their children who are bursting with energy after spending the afternoon cooped up waiting to go out. Now that the boys are older, I can occasionally stay in on my own and read the Sunday papers right through, instead of just having time for the women's pages.

Most of the year, not just in summer, we love to go on picnics. I learnt the knack years ago from a friend who volunteered to prepare the food if I did the driving. When we pulled up in a lay-by, I glanced at what he had brought and thought: 'Well, he hasn't gone to much trouble.' It turned out to be delicious. He unpacked a huge tub of humus, some lovely bread and a big bag of peaches. We sat there dipping and munching in contentment, and washed it down with a bottle of apple juice. He hadn't spent hours wrestling with clingfilm and packing plates, knives and forks, yet it remains one of the most memorable picnics I have had and taught me a lot. There is much to be said for travelling light.

The classic picture of the British family picnic would be funny if it were not for the dampner all those bits of equipment seem to put on the day. Plastic food containers, folding tables, chairs, rugs, crockery, ice-boxes, Primus stoves, kettles and tea-bags – it would be easier to hitch the kitchen to the back of the car. Surely life is formal enough without: 'Sit DOWN! Mind the RUG!' Don't tread on this ... don't tread on that. When you consider what a small proportion of the day is actually spent eating, it makes sense to take as many disposable items as possible. Even rugs are unnecessary if you wear jeans. Once you decide on a ruthless purge, it really is surprising just how little you need. In many ways the traditional English picnic with a small open basket must have been very enjoyable. Sometimes it is fun to prepare things at home, but I keep them to a minimum, perhaps a few tomato or cucumber sandwiches, a bottle of wine, or a flask of tea, and some apples. In winter – one of my favourite seasons for picnics – I take an open-necked flask of soup, or goulash, and some throw-away cups. It keeps your hands warm, but it does make your nose run – so don't forget the tissues!

In the course of hundreds of days out, our staple picnic has whittled itself down to a large, pre-buttered French stick in a throw-away bag, boiled eggs, lumps of cheese, a bag of apples, peaches, plums or whatever happens to be in season, and a bottle of apple juice. Instead of cheese or eggs, I occasionally pack a big pot of pâté, humus or cream cheese, as long as the container is disposable. At the end of the picnic all the wrappings are in the litter bin, my hands are free for the rest of the day and the back of the car does not resemble the scene of a major disaster.

There is something fantastic about going out very early on a fine summer morning as soon as it is light. One of the highlights of our family holidays was to creep out of the house at 5 a.m., and cycle off with a picnic of nuts and dates, freckly bananas and cartons of drinking yoghurt. We rode right through a deserted city centre, where the traffic is normally too heavy, and raced along all the paths you're not allowed on in the park that are normally crammed with visitors. We had the whole place to ourselves, devoured our picnic and went off to feed the ducks. Incidentally, I always take a plastic bag in the bottom of my pannier on bicycle picnics. It is handy to sit on when the grass is wet with early morning dew, and useful for collecting conkers in autumn.

The children love autumn and winter picnics on those cold, dry, crisp days. It is usually too chilly to stay out for long, so we make the picnic a snack rather than a main meal. The nice thing about cold-weather picnics is that you can eat them as you saunter along. Bovril and home-made lemon and honey drinks go down well. I also like to cram in the carbohydrates as the children burn up so much energy running around. A bag of sausage rolls, followed by a large wedge of chocolate cake is their idea of heaven.

VEGETARIAN FOOD

We are not fully-fledged vegetarians, more a pale shade of green. I am not a health food fanatic either, but I do watch what we eat. As a dancer I have never really been a red-meat eater – I used to find it took a long time to digest. Meat and fish do appear on the menu at home, but only in moderation. It is difficult at times to persuade children to eat up their vegetables, and even fruit in some cases. Whenever we have one of those phases, I overcome the problem by cutting a selection of celery or carrots into strips, and leaving them on the table with a bowl of sour cream or cheese dip. They always come home from school starving, ready to eat anything in sight, and will tuck in without hesitation. I also keep a large jug of iced water in the refrigerator. It is infinitely better than orange squash, which is teeming with additives and colouring – paint water I call it.

I have been going to Cranks restaurant since the very first day it opened in Carnaby Street. I was playing opposite Cliff Richard at the Palladium around the corner, and Cliff and Hank Marvin of the Shadows and I used to pop in for tea during rehearsals. In those days I don't think vegetarians watched TV or listened to pop music, so Cliff and Hank weren't even noticed. I also suspect it was because the food was too good to glance up from!

Surrey Raised Pie

One of my favourite meals there was *Surrey Raised Pie*, which was made from hot water crust pastry, savoury mix and sliced tomatoes. The savoury mix is Cranks' answer to vegetarians' need for tasty protein to replace sausage and mincemeats. It makes a perfect filling for pies, pasties and savoury rolls. To make about 1 kg (2 lb) of vegetarian savoury mix you need:

100 g (4 oz) yellow split peas	2 teaspoons yeast extract
1 medium-size carrot	1 tablespoon tomato paste
1 medium-sized onion	1 teaspoon thyme
375 ml ($\frac{3}{4}$ pt) water	1 teaspoon sage
150 g (6 oz) coarse oatmeal	1 tablespoon chopped parsley
1 tablespoon oil	100 g (4 oz) fresh breadcrumbs
2 crushed cloves garlic	salt and pepper to taste

Rinse the yellow split peas and soak them overnight in water.

Grate the carrot and onion and put them, with the peas and water, in a saucepan. Bring to the boil, then cover and simmer for about twenty minutes.

Stir in the oatmeal and cook for a further ten minutes. Take the pan off the heat and add the remaining ingredients. Stir well and leave to cool, before adding seasoning to taste. The result is absolutely delicious.

Hot water crust pastry The nice thing about hot water crust pastry is that it is easy to make, and is especially good for raised savoury pies. Unlike shortcrust pastry, it has a firm texture when taken from the oven. The ingredients, for about 700 g ($1\frac{1}{2}$ lb), are very basic:

450 g (1 lb) 100% wholemeal flour
2 teaspoons salt
100 g (4 oz) white fat
125 ml ($\frac{1}{4}$ pt) milk, or milk and water mixed

My family love to go on picnics. We always travel light, with little more than the food we are going to eat. And we make sure all the containers are disposable so that we don't have to carry anything about with us all day.

Opposite One of my favourite vegetarian recipes is Surrey Raised Pie. It is absolutely delicious served with a mouth-watering tomato sauce and fresh parsley.

Put the fat and milk (or milk and water) into a saucepan and heat until the fat is melted. Mix the flour and salt in a basin, and then pour in the liquid, stirring with a wooden spoon, until the mixture forms a soft dough. Cover the bowl with a damp cloth, or clingfilm, and allow it to rest for half an hour before using.

Line a 14 cm (6 in) diameter, fairly deep cake tin with about three-quarters of the pastry. Spoon half the savoury mix into the base of the tin, smooth it around and top with four sliced tomatoes. Finish-off with a final layer of savory mix.

Roll out the rest of the pastry to make the pie-top, and when you place it in position, seal the edges well and give them a decorative pinch pattern. Make a hole in the centre of the pie, and use the left-over pastry trimmings to make leaves – or something soppy – and arrange them on top.

Bake in the oven at 200°C (400°F/Gas mark 6) for about forty-five minutes. If it appears to be over-browning when you check its progress, cover the pastry with a piece of foil. Leave the pie to cool a little in the tin before serving.

Vegetarian tomato sauce
Absolutely mouth-watering and handy to keep in the refrigerator. To make about 500 ml (1 pt), you need:

1 medium size onion	1 tablespoon tomato paste
350 g (12 oz) tomatoes	$\frac{1}{2}$ teaspoon basil
25 g (1 oz) butter or margarine	salt and pepper to taste
250 ml ($\frac{1}{2}$ pt) vegetable stock, or water	

Chop the onion and the tomatoes, then melt the butter in a saucepan. Throw in the onions and fry them gently until they are transparent; then add the other ingredients. Bring to the boil, then reduce the heat and simmer uncovered for twenty minutes. Serve with savoury pies and rice dishes.

ENTERTAINING FOR WORRIERS

The mere thought of having friends round for a meal, or entertaining visitors, is enough to turn some people to jelly. But not everything you prepare has to be *haute cuisine*. Simple things make the most mouth-watering meals. I remember someone once ringing to say they would be dropping in, and I hadn't anything to give them. I almost got into a state until I looked again at what I had. I made a big bowl of buttery mashed potatoes, boiled up a jar of sauerkraut – cabbage would have done equally well – and decorated the lot with golden-brown bangers. It looked plentiful and appetizing and went down so well. I felt I had really learned something that day. People appreciate simple foods just as much as fancy things, but the trick is to cook it perfectly and serve it lavishly, and with style. There is seldom any waste because, like most housewives, I constantly invent *recherchez* dishes for lunch next day – things like potato cakes with onion rings on top.

People nowadays are so used to convenience foods that, to make an uncomplicated meal such as a large bowl of potato chips, with a plateful of fried eggs and a giant bottle of tomato ketchup, is a pleasant and delicious change. And I use one great lump of Brie, or good cheddar, instead of all those fiddly bits of cheese in tinfoil, or clingfilm, which give you an unwanted nailful of stinky cheese, ponging on the end of your finger all evening.

It also isn't worth giving yourself an ulcer trying to track down exotic fruits – fill a bowl with nothing but tangerines, juicy plums or delicious-looking green apples. It can be just as effective – and does not leave you with doubtful-looking unidentified pieces mouldering in the bottom of the bowl at the end of the evening.

Being on my own, I always seem to waste bottles of wine. When a friend pops in for an hour we rarely manage to drink it all, so lately I've been buying half-bottles of good champagne. Though we have been known to open a second . . . and a third! It's such a treat and, of course, cheaper because there are never any left-overs. If you go to someone's house for dinner and they do it all formally with all the right wines, that's lovely. But if *you* don't like entertaining that way, don't attempt to. Do it your way, and if guests drop in unexpectedly – who says you can't have scrambled eggs with champagne?

57

A Stitch in Time

FAMILY SNACKS

One of our favourites is baked potatoes with a cross cut into the tops, and the flaps turned back with blobs of butter nestling in the centre ... wonderful! I surround the large bowl of potatoes with little ones filled with sour cream and chives, chopped onions, diced bacon and chopped egg, anything which takes our fancy. To add a splash of colour I may put out bowls of sweetcorn, pepper, flaked fish, or pretend caviar. There are so many combinations that we never really tire of baked potatoes.

When I don't want to go to the shops we have Fridge Scrape, made up from everything we can find in the cupboard or fridge – it is one of the boys' favourites. You can make soup from all kinds of vegetables, and fruit salad from the left-over fruit. All the odds and ends of cheese can be grated into a bowl to sprinkle on the soup, and a big jug of custard uses up any milk or cream which may be left.

One quick and easy snack, which is a favourite of mine, is a mixture of muffins, poached eggs, sliced ham and hollandaise sauce. I grill the muffins, pull them open and cover them with a slice of ham. The poached eggs go on top, with a big blob of hollandaise sauce to finish it off. I prepare the sauce first and, as it musn't go cold, I keep it in a wide-necked vacuum flask ready to use.

Hollandaise sauce

3 egg yolks	2 tablespoons wine vinegar
100 g (4 oz) butter	pinch of salt and pepper

I put the egg yolks and vinegar in the top of a double saucepan, and stir them together well. Then I add some hot, but not boiling, water into the bottom section of the double saucepan, and heat the yolks slowly until the mixture thickens. As it is warming I add a small piece of butter and whisk it in gently until it melts. Then I add the rest of the butter, a little at a time, whisking until the sauce thickens. I add the salt and pepper at the end, when the pan is off the heat, and serve warm.

When the sauce is prepared, I toast the muffins while the eggs are poaching. I never use a proper tin for poached eggs because, frankly, I find them boring. I cook the eggs in fast-boiling water in an ordinary saucepan with a splodge of vinegar, remembering to turn down the heat before tipping them in. When they are done I scoop them out with a slatted spoon. Prepared in the right sequence, the snack is quick and comes together easily for serving.

One of our favourite Saturday-morning-slopping-around snacks is a large jug of chilled apple juice, a basketful of piping hot croissants and a great hunk of fresh Brie – a delicious combination.

Chocolate Sauce
We all love ice cream with hot chocolate sauce. There are lots of smart sauces for ice cream, but this one is like serving a big jug of fancy custard. Incidentally, it's odd, you know, that a large jug of custard goes down better with my friends than fresh cream does. It must be something to do with memories of schooldays! You need:

> 500 ml (½ pt) milk
> 1 tablespoon cornflour
> drinking chocolate

Blend the cornflour with a little milk in a cup while the rest of the milk is coming up to the boil in the pan. When it is smooth, add it to the milk in the pan. As the mixture is cooking nicely, stir in the drinking chocolate to suit your taste. A blob of cream, or butter, makes it richer and smoother.

CHILDREN'S PARTIES

It is easy to get just as flustered organizing children's parties as when entertaining grown-ups. Once you have made your lists and decided what to do, the secret is to believe in yourself. I love to turn everyday meals with the children into an impromptu party. As they enjoy surprises, I sometimes serve the pudding first, just for a change, and to relieve the monotony of meal times. If they have brought friends home I dish out jam roly-poly, then I hold the jug up high, out of sight, and pour bright green custard over it. You should see their faces. (I make it, incidentally, from pure vegetable colouring, not chemical food dye.)

There are endless possibilities with food colouring. I enjoy secretly putting a drop or two in the bottom of their glasses. When you pour out the lemonade it instantly changes colour, and their faces light up.

Parties can be expensive, I suppose, if you have to keep buying cups, and cloths with comic characters on, and all the other throw-away paraphernalia. Years ago I invested in a set of bright yellow tin mugs and plates, and a red and yellow table-cloth. They have not only lasted, but we use them for all sorts of other occasions as well.

One of our party favourites is to take an orange, cut it in half, and squeeze the juice into a basin. I then scoop out the pithy bits and tidy up the insides. I use the juice from the orange to make a jelly and pour it carefully into the orange-peel cups. When they have set in the fridge – on a foil tray in case they spill – I cut them into slices to make them look like real oranges again. The children love them, and they are getting all the goodness of the orange in a gimmicky form. You can also make them look like little boats with rice paper sails and a wooden toothpick for a mast.

When mums are out at work it is often difficult to throw a children's party in the afternoon, or even at tea-time, because of all the preparation. Birthdays are very special to children, and I hate them to fall flat or be a disappointment. Recently, when I knew I had little time, I got them up very early for breakfast, daddy arrived in his evening suit and we had the whole caboodle before school. All that party fare for breakfast, with both parents in evening dress, delighted them.

I think that sometimes it is really good to be a bit daft with your children. Don't worry if you go too far – they are sure to let you know in no uncertain terms if you are being a show-off. Occasionally at their parties I used to announce to all the assembled children: 'Oh, we'll all have to go outside – it's raining!' They would stare blankly until my own children, suspecting something was afoot, led the charge into the garden. Once they were outdoors, I would race upstairs and shower them with buckets of sweets from the bedroom window.

THE WAY WE WERE

'*A breakfast-table barometer:* A cup of hot coffee is an unfailing barometer, if you allow a lump of sugar to drop to the bottom of the cup and watch the air bubbles arise without disturbing the coffee. If the bubbles collect in the middle, the weather will be fine; if they adhere to the cup, forming a ring, it will either rain or snow; and if the bubbles separate without assuming any fixed position, changeable weather may be expected ...'

ON BEING A
SINGULAR PARENT

ONE OF MY children's favourite authors is Roald Dahl. They used to ask me anxiously: 'He's not dead, is he, Mum? I couldn't bear it if he didn't write any more stories.' I had been reading *Danny The Champion Of The World* to them, and later I remembered the message at the end of the book:

> When you grow up
> and have children of your own
> do please remember something important
> a stodgy parent is no fun at all
> What a child wants
> and deserves
> is a parent who is
> S P A R K Y

As I was going through a rather drippy phase it quite inspired me. That week we were having a children's birthday party, and I had an ideal opportunity to introduce myself as a sparky parent. I was driving home after picking all the children up from school, and we found ourselves in a street where the traffic was quiet, so I stopped the car. When they all asked what the problem was, I told them we would have to wait because there was an elephant crossing the road. Then I stuck my hand out of the window and started banging on the roof to get rid of the monkeys. They all joined in enthusiastically, and by the time I had pretended to have forgotten where we lived, swerving in and out of the drives of strange houses, they were howling with laughter.

At the party, the cake was in vibrant colours, I was tossing sweets from the bedroom windows, sweating with the effort of it all, but hugging myself for such a sparky performance. When it was all over, I asked them breathlessly: 'Was it great? Did you love it?' And they chorused: 'Oh Mum – it was nearly ruined! You were such a show-off!' . . . So I just went back to being a drip.

It is important to lark around with your children, like romping with a puppy, as well as being fierce. They love the attention and the affection. If you suddenly start being silly it embarrasses them at first, but when they become used to it they don't feel bad at all. Except, of course, if they are teenagers – then you are not allowed to do anything! Or at least, nothing you do is right. It isn't even all right to be brilliant: 'Why can't you be thick, like other parents?'

The first signs begin to appear years before: 'Why can't you have a scrubbed face like my friend's mummy?' I remember picking up one of my boys from school when I happened to be wearing a rather posh cross-over cardigan with a matching beret. It wasn't an over-the-top hat, but I wore it on the side and thought I looked quite good in it. He came out of school, took one look at me and turned purple. All the way home he seemed to be walking about a mile behind me whispering: 'Oh my God, oh my God!'

When we got in the house he said in anguish: '. . . and Sam saw you too – with your hat on!'

I replied rather tentatively: 'Would you like me to look like Sam's mother, then?'

And he chewed it over and said: 'Well sometimes, yes.'

I must admit I had a few giggles over that when I wondered what Sam must have been saying to *his* mum at the same time.

Being a single parent can be difficult. You have to rely on your own judgment from day to day, wondering if you are doing the right thing with no one to help, or back you up. I've often wished that there was a little book I could open which would tell me: today you do this, tomorrow you do that. . . .

When my oldest son reached adolescence, I remember thinking: if only someone had told me. It all seemed so foreign that one day I took out the encyclopaedia and looked up the word. The gist of it, I recall, was that if this happened at any other age, it would be considered madness. It gave me great comfort and made me think that, after all, it is nothing new and has been going on for generations. It doesn't stop you, of course, dreading who they might meet around the corner. All you can do is put them on the rungs of the ladder, but it does seem that there is such a long way to fall. A few generations ago parents worried about their sons in the war; we have sleepless nights about drugs, rapes and muggings. All you can do is put in a lot of work, and pray for the best. There is a lovely saying in *Quotations From The Prophet*, by Kahlil Gibran: 'Your children are only on hire . . .' Which is so true, but if only they knew the hell we go through making the payments. I never feel smug or superior if someone else's child gets into trouble, because you just don't know how yours will cope. So I now just enjoy the lulls between the storms, and think of it as the heaven and hell of child-caring.

Most children go through the funny clothes and hair stage. I remember when my eldest started – out of the blue – wearing an old band-leader's jacket and trousers made from black-out material.

We went on a really swish holiday where the hotel floors were all marble and everybody paraded round in their silks in the evening. We had all changed for dinner and were walking across to the restaurant, where a man in a dinner-jacket was waiting to show us to our seats. I arrived first with Jason behind me, squelching across the marble floor in a pair of enormous brothel-creepers. Punk had only just hit London, never mind abroad, and all the Swiss and Germans were staring at him open-mouthed. He had dyed his hair navy blue and teased it into a style which looked like a raven perching on his head. I distinctly recall sitting down with everyone looking at me, obviously thinking: 'Oh, that poor woman!'

I plunged into some dreadful acting, looking light-heartedly around saying: 'Isn't this WONDERFUL?' While all the time I was cringing inside thinking: 'I wish he had a grey flannel suit. WHY isn't he in a grey flannel suit?' I felt embarrassed, but I was determined not to let them know – and I wasn't going to let my son know either. I respected his need to express how he felt. Now, as it happens, he has bought himself a grey flannel suit – which he wears with Bob Geldorf whiskers. I was lucky really, I suppose, because the outrageous outfits only lasted a year, even if it did feel like a lifetime. Now he's done it, and hopefully he won't be into medallions and Cuban-heeled boots when he's forty.

The only thing I could do about it at the time was to ensure that whenever the funny clothes hit the floor, which was often, they were in the washing-machine and ironed before you could blink. Even though they were huge and baggy, they were squeaky clean and had amazing creases. There are so many things to say 'No' to – or, 'Please don't, I'd rather you didn't' – that, if it's harmless, it's best to keep your tongue between your teeth. There are worse things than dressing up in the latest fashions.

One of my son's best friends lived in the country, and whenever we visited his family they'd smile sympathetically and say: 'We're *so* lucky living out here and missing all this.' But of course their smile slipped, because their son did everything exactly the same, but it hit him much later. We all think we are going to escape, but not many do.

It is so much better to look funny at fourteen than at forty. I recall a friend of mine absolutely screaming at his son because he had printed, very neatly, on an old leather jacket: Adam Ant. It was beautifully done in small, white painted letters across the upper sleeve. He was roaring and shouting: 'Get that jacket off – it looks disgusting!' While all the time he was sitting there with two 10 cm (4 in) high, brass 'G's, for Gucci, on his belt buckle. Quite honestly, I couldn't see the difference.

Parents who agonize about 'problem teenagers' often forget that they are probably at a problem age themselves. By the time our children are in their teens, most of us are heading towards middle age, and it is just possible that the awkwardness is not one-sided. The forties are an age when boredom, dissatisfaction, and over-work can become immense burdens. It is a time when people look forward and don't necessarily like what they see. When youth has gone, and confidence is often just out of reach, our own insecurity can make us critical, snappy, demanding and over-protective.

Because I appear on television, I am occasionally invited onto other people's shows and find myself asked to air my views on single parenthood. It can be quite embarrassing because, as anyone who is a parent knows, family life changes all the time. We are constantly reviewing our attitudes and position as our children grow older, developing their characters and individual needs. What may have been true for years suddenly changes, and we find we have to change with it. Single parenthood is almost a fashionable topic nowadays, but it is nothing new really. Forty years ago, with dad off to war, the country was full of millions of mums trying to cope single-handed and often in real poverty, without any help from Supplementary Benefits.

Interviewers usually follow-up with the inevitable question: 'Yes, but of course, Una, you have no financial worries.' This implies that however well I've coped is irrelevant, because we are now more comfortably placed. It's true that I have been lucky in finding a job that I can fit in with bringing up a family. And I have also been lucky that my career has not suffered beyond repair because I haven't been able to devote all my time to it. But, at the end of the day, I do work hard, and I have to support my family and the home we live in.

None of this, of course, gets to the heart of the matter, which is the emotional side. When a marriage goes wrong you have to come to terms with a sense of loss, and in some cases rejection. Learning to be strong without being domineering is the first tentative step towards self-confidence. It is a long, hard journey becoming a whole person again, wounded but not broken. It is a lot easier to talk about such things in retrospect, but I don't think one ever forgets the panic and self-doubts. I hope, however, that I am now a better woman for it, more tolerant and sympathetic. I have also learned to accept that parents can't always assume the blame for every single thing. It may be a natural, instinctive reaction, but it places an unnecessary burden both on you and the children.

When my children were babies I wanted to wrap them in cotton wool and wake them up when they were twenty-one. This was closely followed by the stage when I wished *I* could be wrapped up in cotton wool until *they* were twenty-one. It's silly, of course, and somehow or other you manage to cope. Although we seldom have control over what happens to us, I do believe the old saying that God helps those who help themselves. I have come to rely pretty heavily on being organized, not round the clock, but in a general, determined way throughout the year. I discipline myself to sort out my wardrobe for the seasons, for instance. Of course, clothes are important in my job, but I believe that no matter what a woman does, she feels more relaxed if she is happy and comfortable with what she is wearing.

When children are very young there are times when you can't help feeling harassed, or even trapped in the house. Unfortunately, by the time you get babies dressed and ready to go out, it is almost time to come home again. I would drop everything I was doing, wash my hair, put on some make-up and wear, not just any old thing, but something which made me feel good. I would take them out and make myself say 'hello' to people, even if it meant getting into conversation about someone's dog. It can be a great effort to make friends after having a baby. It isn't that all your friends have deserted you, but it seems as though everyone else is always out at work. I enjoyed going to the local shop rather than the supermarket, so that I could have a chat. It cheered me up immensely. There was nowhere to go in the area where I lived, but I was lucky enough to have a car, so I would head for Golders Green where there is a nice park with people milling around. I am excruciatingly shy, but I used to make a great effort to pretend myself out of it.

The trouble with having a baby is that you are always so tired that you often put off getting back into shape. Some people are lucky and all the fat just burns off, but I think most of us have to work at it.

I remember being very chubby and walking down the King's Road – I was 14 st when I was pregnant, and 10 st after I'd had Joe. I looked at slim women and thought: 'Huh, it's all right for them!' Finally I had to give myself a sharp lecture: 'You haven't got a hump, or a false leg you know. There isn't a bad shape underneath all this flab, so it's up to you.' And I really did it – the secret is, you have to want to.

It is no good being negative, saying: 'I wish I could, but . . .' Time passes by and you spend your life being discontented. I have stopped wishing for something I don't really want, or else I have a darned good try at it. So often it is the trying that counts. Not everyone is a success at everything, but you can enjoy being a pretty keen amateur.

Sometimes it is better to discard hard-and-fast rules and follow your own lifestyle, like ditching Sunday lunch and having a whole day out with the children. I find, too, that it is important to share troubles as well as joys with them. I know lots of people who say: 'Don't tell the children,' but occasionally it helps.

A week or so before Christmas I had the monthly curse. As it often makes me feel quite ill, I thought: 'Well, they're old enough, I'll explain what is affecting me.' They were very understanding, and disappeared upstairs in a rush of giggles to talk about it. Then just days before Christmas, when I was very busy and looking more than a little harassed sorting things out, my youngest came to me and asked earnestly: 'Mum, have you got the curse again?' He is now convinced it's something I have every time I'm ratty!

It is nice to confide in your children. If you are close to them, as I am, they know if something is wrong, anyway, no matter how well you try to cover up. Children are very sensitive and rely a great deal on their instincts. When you insist that there is nothing wrong, but they know there is, they tend to carry round a burden of guilt, thinking it's their fault. It is also confusing and a little hurtful to be shut out from you. If it happens too often, then one day they may not come to you with their problems, which would be awful. I think sharing our problems makes us more tolerant and understanding towards each other. I have talked many things over with my boys, and their sympathy and understanding has been an enormous comfort – not to mention their very forthright advice! I have seen the notion of 'protecting' the children backfire on parents when their sons and daughters become selfishly preoccupied with themselves and disinterested in other people's problems.

While children can understand many things, I do not believe in filling them up with information they cannot absorb, like explaining the complete sex act to them when they are four. But their emotions are so wide open that talking things through with them really does help. They may, for instance, feel guilty that daddy has left, and blame themselves. I understand this is quite a common reaction, but it is terrible for them to misunderstand like that.

Whenever children ask outright questions I answer simply and within reason, but keep things on a need-to-know basis. I never embroider, or go on too long – if they want to know more, they'll ask another question. I try to be matter-of-fact because if I become tongue-tied with embarrassment, rather than remaining completely natural, they would go to someone else. And I'd rather it came from me. Bedtime is usually the time they want to talk or tell me things, if only to put off having to go to sleep. Even if they have nothing particular to say they will dredge up something. When I 'tour the dorms' I like to spend a little time individually with them. It is easy to lump them together as 'the children', but they are individuals, first and foremost.

There inevitably comes a time when the chatter subsides. They reach the age when they don't want to talk when they come in from school – which is exactly how grown-ups feel when they arrive home from work. They want a little time to themselves, knowing that you are there if they feel like talking.

The greatest gift you can give your children is in having the strength to let them go. It is hard, but it happens to us all. 'Your child is like an arrow shot from your bow,' it has been said. The day soon comes when they walk down the drive forgetting to blow you a kiss. It does hurt a little, but it is tremendously rewarding to see them gaining confidence and learning to stand on their own feet: the first step to becoming a complete person. Never spoil the moment by reminding them that they have forgotten to kiss you or, worse still, pulling a long face to make them feel guilty. Being a martyr is your problem, not theirs.

I do think boys prepare you for it earlier than girls, if only because of their embarrassment at being kissed in public. Teenagers can worry about their parents, particularly if they are single parents, but I am already making plans about what I am going to do when they grow up. I hope to be an independent, adventurous, eccentric old lady, probably pausing with my grandchildren to allow elephants to cross the road . . . it's the very least I can do for them.

THE WAY WE WERE

'*Toothache:* Electrify the teeth by applying a magnet, or lay roasted parings of turnips, as hot as can be, behind the ear. It is also effective to keep the feet in warm water, and rub them well with bran, just before bedtime.'

'*Stitch in the side:* Apply treacle spread on brown paper.'

'*Whitlow:* Cut a hole in a lemon and wear it on the affected finger like a thimble until cured . . .'

WISH YOU
WERE HERE

I LOVE THE whole ceremony of preparing and leaving for holidays, there is such an air of bustle and excitement. Packing requires strong self-control, especially when it comes to children, who always want to take their entire toy-room with them. I solved the problem by buying each of them a strong, light back-pack, into which they can jam their cards, pencils and toys. If they put too much in, they soon find that that's their problem – next year they won't want to be leaning backwards everywhere they walk.

The same applies to grown-ups, too. It is so tempting to take too much. Even if you are going somewhere where everyone changes in the evening, resist it. Be confident and take just a couple of things you can swop around to make different outfits, instead of something new for every night. I remember one holiday where there was a stunningly beautiful woman who wore the same dress every single evening. She was obviously rinsing it out like fury, but she looked amazing.

A list is useful for all those things you tend to leave at home (the children, for instance!).

When your holiday wardrobe is laid out on the bed, ruthlessly whittle it down to what you really need and are sure to wear. Wrap the things you decide upon carefully in tissue so that everything arrives fresh and does not need ironing. The secret of having crease-free clothes is also not to over-pack or under-pack.

I always put towels in the bottom of my case, along with heavy items, and stack my folded clothes in the centre. I arrange my shirts and blouses top-to-toe to avoid creasing the collars. Round the edges I fill the gaps with tights, bras, knickers and socks to stop the clothes sliding around. At the hotel I fold all the tissue wrapping and stow it away to use again.

If you are staying in a posh hotel, and are completely overawed, don't forget that most of the other guests probably have the same feeling too! Try to do everything positively, even the littlest things, as this will help you to pull them off with style. You can eat with your fingers, as long as you do it with confidence. When you look around and think: 'Oh, it's all right for them, they're so self-assured,' remember that most people, at some time or another, are putting on an act to cover terrible inhibitions or shyness. There's nothing wrong, for instance, in not knowing how to tackle an unusual dish. It's far better to ask than worry about how to attack it without it leaping into your lap. Eating should be fun, and it is a great shame to stifle good conversation and a relaxed atmosphere by getting into a state over bits of cutlery.

When we have really hot weather on holiday, the children often get bored with swimming every day. Last summer, after our early morning breakfast picnic, I took them to see two films in one day. Parents get so used to demanding: 'What are you children doing indoors on a blazing hot day?', that it feels quite decadent to sneak off to the matinee, have something to eat and then go back again. And the children were quite tickled to go, not once, but twice on a really hot day. And, for me, sitting in the cool cinema made a refreshing change.

Let's be honest, the annual desperate quest for a holiday tan is rather boring. And unless you have lovely silky Continental skin, the damage can last a lifetime. Sunbathing only became fashionable because to have a tan suggested you could afford a summer holiday. As most people can now afford to travel, or at least hire a sunbed, it's quite naff really. To sit in dappled light in the shade of a tree, with sun and haze all around you, is beautiful – and much better for you too. You can sew, read a book without being half-blinded, or just watch the world go by. All that performance of rubbing sandy oil over yourself, and that dreadful lobster period when no one can go near you because you're so violently red and sore, makes me shudder, as I remember it well. I decided that, although I do love the sunshine, I wouldn't let it ruin my skin anymore. What's wrong with smooth, white legs anyway? It's far better to be cool and pale-skinned than to be red, peeling and looking like an extra from *The Towering Inferno*. I have seen some quite nasty-looking burns being paraded as suntan. If the sun affects you, it is common sense to protect your skin and keep it in good condition for as long as you can. You have only to turn your arms over to feel the difference in the texture of skin which is not exposed to the weather.

As we get older, I suppose we notice these things more. Skin that is always in the sunlight becomes quite crêpey, while more protected areas, like thighs and breasts, remain softer and silkier. The back of one

71

of my hands is covered with liver spots, but the other isn't. For a long time I couldn't understand why, until I realized that it is the hand which is always on top when I am stitching. The same hand also gets the sunlight through the open car window when I am driving. A 'mole-doctor' recently told me that the French call liver spots 'medals for age'. Some people get them, he said, and some don't, but you are less likely to get them if you keep your hands out of the sun; which probably explains why ladies used to wear summer gloves and wide-brimmed hats and carried parasols.

Winter holidays can provide some of the best comedy turns of the year. I once sat in an airport in Switzerland, stuffing a handkerchief into my mouth, because the whole scene around me was like some ridiculous joke. The people who didn't have broken limbs all had purple faces with big white patches, as though they were still wearing goggles. I suppose some people aren't as vain as I am, and don't care what they look like. I'm sure they could all limp off looking like exploded plums and say: 'Oh, we had a *super* time!'

Perhaps we need all these funny sports, and aerobics and jogging because we are not doing all the old-fashioned things like walking, scrubbing and brushing. Labour-saving gadgets have taken the exercise out of housework, so now we have to throw ourselves into some sport or other to stave-off kimono arms and wobbly thighs. There is an air of panic about it all.

THE WAY WE WERE

'*Headache from heat:* To prevent heat affecting the head in summer, place a cabbage leaf or a large lettuce leaf in your hat. It will keep the head cool . . .'

'*Bugs:* Persons who travel often meet with these vermin, and are sadly bitten by them. To prevent this, let your nightshirt be washed as ordinarily, well-wrung, and then dipped in a solution of alum, or camphor, and then allowed to dry. A sure preventative . . .'

'*Damp beds:* To ascertain if beds are damp, place a looking-glass between the sheets for a few minutes. If upon its removal the glass be clouded, it is better for the traveller to put up with the discomfort of sleeping in the blankets, than stand the chance of catching cold, or rheumatism.'

'*Seasickness:* If in dread of seasickness, lie down on the back at least a quarter of an hour before the vessel starts. No other position will do. Let the head, body and back become, as it were, part of the vessel, participating in its motion without any muscular effort. In some time you will begin to feel that you can swallow a little champagne and water . . .'

When the Nights are Drawing In...

GLAD ALL OVER

THE MERE THOUGHT of sport, or jogging, or aerobics gives me a strong urge to lie down in a darkened room. Most of my exercise is done running up and down stairs at home, but I do enjoy walking and swimming. They provide marvellous overall exercise. If you are angry, especially, there is nothing quite like striding out and stamping along the pavement. Health is really little more than an acquired habit. If you make a point of not slouching along, for instance, then no matter how bad you feel, you still stand straight and hold yourself well.

There is, however, the constant lure of organized health, and I must confess to momentary weakness. My friend, actress Julia McKenzie, and I decided to splash out and join the Sanctuary in Covent Garden which is, I suppose, the ultimate ladies' health retreat. It conjures images of pillared calm, palm trees, parakeets, lazy ambling cats, women plunging healthily into a sumptuous swimming-pool and swinging languidly above the water on a flower-entwined trapeze. A wonderful place for the worn-out woman and the generally jaded business gel. You can lounge around for the whole day having facials, massage, pedicures or unashamedly snoozing.

One tiny problem Julia and I hadn't discussed with each other was the abundance of nudity. We have both shared dressing-rooms for years, but somehow neither of us got around to actually mentioning what – if anything – we would wear. It was, after all, the ultimate opportunity to shed the mantle of daily care and tiptoe carefree through the palm trees. We disappeared into our respective changing rooms and emerged, simultaneously, in thick serge, floor-length gowns, like a couple of sanitorium patients on the run. We exchanged sideways glances at the identical outfits, like two old dears draped from neck to toe in asylum chic.

Trying desperately to put a carefree spring in our steps, and look anything but prudish, we sidled into the jacuzzi and primly squeezed among the acres of naked flesh. All around women lounged luxuriously with their breasts bobbing just above the water line, as we sat uncomfortably until an appropriate length of time had passed. If we had kept our watches on, I'm sure we would have been glancing at them.

Next we squelched to the swimming-pool, lowering ourselves in gingerly, and on to dry off in the sauna, clutching our white sanitorium day-wear around us. The more we tried to slink inconspicuously round the poolside, the more we made a spectacle of ourselves. Being swathed from head to foot amid such uninhibited nakedness made me feel almost obscene.

The Sanctuary really is a wonderful place, more spectacular even than its members. It soars in classical splendour, while all around they lie exhausted. Judging by the number of women snoring in chairs, with breasts gently aquiver, it is most relaxing. You feel that if you don't walk about looking like something out of a Bond film, you really are lowering the tone of the place. So far, unfortunately, our first foray into total health had proved remarkably anxiety-ridden.

The only sensible answer was a massage. It meant reluctantly taking our clothes off – even the experts at the Sanctuary would find it a stiff test pummelling through armour-plated serge – but if I didn't go home feeling at least a little relaxed, I would feel I hadn't had my money's worth.

Our mistake was bad timing. We decided to go after the salad lunch, which is an obligatory part of the visit, and all the elaborate care taken to make clients feel blissfully at ease was as much use as a button on a hat. In the massage room the lights are lowered and women slip effortlessly into sleep as their weary bodies are slapped and squeezed. I managed to get hiccups, which refused to go away. In the gently-lit room, while all around us were asleep, I lay there going hic ... hic ... hic ... with a lump of carrot caught in my windpipe. No doubt, too,

there was a piece of lettuce stuck to my teeth.

At the end of the massage, the girl cooed quietly in my ear: 'Did you go to sleep?' But I was so exhausted, all I could manage was a faint 'No'. The problem was that the whole place is so splendid you feel a compulsion to be very serious, and to the manner born. It was only outside that Julia and I discovered that we had both lain there rigid in fear of farting. All those healthy greens followed by that vigorous pounding and pressing of air-pockets made it an extremely risky business. We had each tightly clenched our buttocks, praying that nothing unthinkable would liberate itself in the masseuse's face.

When I got home my eldest son wanted to know if I had enjoyed it. I showed him the brochure, hoping he wouldn't notice how much it had cost. He looked at me, as only sons can, and said: 'You should go more often Mum – don't you think you deserve it?'

Looking back, I suppose the giggling did me more good than the treatment. There is nothing quite like a smile for chasing away the blues. I thought it a good idea when someone declared a Smiling Week. I know we shouldn't go round grinning at everybody, but it drew attention to the point that you have to go out to people. Sometimes it means having to smile first, which can be difficult if you are crippled with shyness, as I am. Then it really becomes a matter of self-training.

We can all get so involved in our own affairs that it becomes too much of an effort to pass on a kind word. It really is a great shame, because a smile or a cheery word can give people such a lift. If your bus conductor is grumpy in the morning it almost puts a blight on the whole day. When he is bright and cheerful, you get a good feeling.

I was shopping in Marks and Spencer recently, when I noticed a foreign woman, who obviously did not know me, looking at what I was wearing. I smiled at her, and she came over to me and said: 'Excuse me, but I think you are very pretty.' I felt embarrassed, and said thank you. When I got home I thought: 'Well, perhaps I don't look so bad!' I sat there glowing, thinking how kind she was to make a nice remark.

Letter-writing is another example. It requires effort, but it means so much to people that it is worth turning it into an enjoyable art. Everyone I know would certainly prefer to get letters, rather than just bills, in the post. There is something rather special about buying yourself a really good fountain-pen and some beautiful paper. The shops have so many lovely sets, that the only difficulty is choosing between them. In this hi-tech age it is a pleasure to receive a hand-written letter. Whenever I receive letters which have to be answered, I put them in a case with my writing materials, and make the time once a week to reply to them all.

One of my sons always found it difficult to write neatly (I should have sent him for hand-writing lessons, because he is such a perfectionist – if he can't do it well, then he won't do it at all). Recently he had a business letter to write and doggedly refused all offers of help. 'It has to be in a man's words, Mum, not a woman's,' he said with great independence. He bought some nice note-paper and a fountain-pen and sat down to work on it. At the end he was immensely proud of his results. It really is worth the effort – throw away those biros and buy yourself a fountain-pen!

People sometimes say to me: 'Oh, you always look so happy, Una.' Well, I'm not always, but I don't believe in whingeing in public. I can be miserable too, and I do have a melancholy side, as most people do. However, I am actually paid to look cheerful; it is part of the job.

I am a firm believer in that old song: 'Make believe you're brave, and the trick will take you far – you may be as brave as you make believe you are.' Like many other people, I have had awful times in my life, some of which I certainly could not go through again. But I don't believe you should foist that onto the world in general. It is something for me alone to cope with, or sort out with close friends. I hate sounding worthy, but it is true that if you care about other people's feelings, you forget about your own – or at least sit on them for a while.

Sometimes it is hard not to sink into a gloom when things are bad, but at the end of the day it's up to you. I have learnt that only I can pull myself up by my bootstraps. Some things, such as grief, do take time, but one should never feel guilty or try to rush what is really a natural process. Just as it takes time to heal, it takes time to cope too.

I remember talking with a friend and telling him that I felt guilty because I was depressed. I was going on about being comfortably off and having no right to feel down, when he said: 'Look Una, just because the Queen's got Buck House doesn't mean she never gets miserable.'

I do think that sharing problems with a close friend or a neighbour can really help. But when it comes to the end, to tying it up and putting it away, then only you can do that. And it is impossible unless you give yourself time, like going for a walk, or sitting quietly and thinking things out. It is especially important if you are overworked, or over-tired, because that is when problems grow out of proportion.

For a long time I couldn't understand why so many men disappear into the loo with a book for hours on end. It is one way of switching off and locking the door on the world. Setting yourself time aside to think is important. I value solitude, I suppose, because I came from a large family, and went from there into the chatter and bustle of the chorus,

When I am on my own I enjoy listening to the radio, especially Radio 4 which introduced me to the pleasures of classical music. Now I keep a note-book and pen by the radio to jot down the name of a piece of music I particularly enjoy as I hear it.

and then into films. Whenever I have a day with crowds of people around, I try to grab ten minutes for myself, just to be alone. I treasure it so much partly because it was a long time before I had the luxury of my own dressing-room.

In recent years I have abandoned the loo for Radio 4, which I thoroughly enjoy. Radio 4 introduced me to classical music, and I am learning more about it all the time. I like Sibelius, and the English School – Delius, Elgar, Vaughan Williams. When the children are out I turn up the radio until the vases bounce, especially with Sibelius. I find myself throwing out my arms in the crescendos. If the children ever walked in they would be saying: 'Turn that row down!'

I like to keep a note-book and pen by the radio for Richard Baker's programme, *Baker's Dozen*. Then, if there is something I like, I buy the tape and play it in the car until I am familiar with it. When I am driving alone, I like to put on a cassette without looking at the box, to see how long it takes me to identify it.

As I do not come from a classical music background, I try to encourage my children to appreciate it in a natural fashion. I would never dream of pretentiously forcing hours and hours of classical music on them, but if children are surrounded by it from being tiny, it becomes a familiar friend. At a certain age most of them are guaranteed to go: 'Ugh! Classical music!' But if it has been played at home, and they recognize a phrase in a TV film, or a commercial, it's surprising how quickly they say: 'Oh, I like this one!' I don't, of course, enjoy everything I hear, but exploring new things is all part of becoming your own person.

When I was trying to come to terms with being a single parent, I remember saying something like: 'I don't know what's in this for me.' My sister, who is my dearest friend, snapped: 'Nothing if you don't get your finger out!' And really it was just the jolt I needed. She helped me get up again. I forced myself to have a dinner party, with just close friends at first, each month, and I promised myself that if there was one thing I wasn't going to do, it was talk about my problems. When you are depressed it is all too easy to do nothing, which only makes things worse. Organizing the dinner party forced me to keep my mind off myself, and listening to others helped me to realize that I wasn't the only one with things on my mind.

Friends are very important to me. Sometimes it is difficult to make friends, but I think if you try to be a friend – rather than sitting there waiting to be approached – it is truly worthwhile. My shyness problem is difficult to overcome, but I have found a strength in me that I never knew I had. It is like opening a cupboard and finding a lump of it there waiting for me to use.

To be outgoing and pretend I am not shy requires all my acting skills. The dreadful thing is that it catches you unawares sometimes. Certain types of people can make you shy, and if they are super-intellectual, they can be overawing. A friend of mine is married to Benny Green, who is an absolutely brilliant man, and I once asked her how she coped with erudite guests. Her solution, when she is not *au fait* with a particular conversation, is to listen. So now, if a conversation moves out of my own experience or knowledge, I do the same. I have found that my interest can be sparked by diverse subjects, which I sometimes go on to explore with books at home. I have long since stopped thinking that I should know everything, but I can do people the courtesy of listening to what they have to say.

When I was young, I dreaded being forty, but little did I know then how contented I would be. I have earned my resilience and independence, and learned to stand or fall by my own efforts. At forty-seven I can now appreciate my good points as well as my bad ones, and accept myself for what I am. I am always planning new adventures for when I get older. I draw great inspiration from an old lady on *Woman's Hour* who sits in Gatwick Airport waiting for the last-minute opportunity for a cheap, or even free, seat somewhere. Sometimes it is to Rome for the day, or Warsaw and back for tea. Life is as exciting as you wish to make it.

I have a wonderful friend, Lucy Morgan, who presented a programme with me on TVS. She is the kindest, most outgoing, adorable person, yet she has had some awful problems. When I asked her how she manages to look so cheerful – why her mouth isn't down in her shoes – she told me: 'I was just lucky. I happened to read a book which said you have a choice. Either you blame everybody for the rest of your life for what happened in your childhood, or a broken marriage, or you can say "No, that was in the past, and now it's up to me."' She decided not to drag her past into the future, and because of it she is a remarkable person.

When I was a small girl my parents used to buy me Alison Uttley books, which I loved. The pictures in them lived with me – everything was made to look so cosy. There was always a cheery fire and the houses were neat and homely.

In my chorus days of digs and bedsits, my sole burning ambition was to keep warm. In the mornings I used to call for my friend, who lived in digs up the road, and we would walk to the Tube together. One morning she was not outside, and I looked through the window to see her lighting her paraffin heater, so the room would be warm when she returned from work. It made a lasting impression on me. While lots of people in my line of work were struggling to become successful, or famous, my only ambition was to be able to afford to leave my paraffin heater on all day. I had to light mine when I got home, and stand in front of it to thaw out.

I now have an open fire, which I can never take for granted after years of digs. I can never forget standing shivering on a soggy, squelching bath mat which had more water in it than we were allowed in the bath. The carpet was so greasy that you had to hold onto the wall when you walked round the room.

The highlight was at the end of the week when we moved to another theatre and everyone changed trains at Crewe. Choruses from all the different shows would be waving to each other like mad across the platforms, with the respective stars standing some distance away down the platform, surrounded by expensive luggage and looking aloof.

THE WAY WE WERE

'*Hysterics:* This disease mostly affects young, nervous single women. It manifests itself by fits, palpitations, a rumbling in the bowels, laughing, crying, and the sensation of a ball rising in the throat.

A vapour bath should be given as soon as possible: sit naked upon a chair and place the legs upon a stool. Throw a large blanket around the patient, pin it under her chin and make it tight all around. Place a vessel under the chair, containing hot water and a mixture of bitter herbs. Heat a couple of bricks until red hot and place them in the mixture. Add about three pints of boiling water and a gill of strong vinegar. When the bricks have cooled, apply friction to the patient with rough towels dipped in vinegar and water. The benefits are immense . . .'

'*Health:* Ladies should defy the bad weather with the use of stout walking boots, a large thick cloak, and an umbrella, and walk two miles every day. Keep your mouth closed and walk rapidly. The air can only reach the lungs by a circuit of the nose and head, and becomes warm before reaching the lungs, thus causing no derangement. Neglect of these precautions brings sickness and death to multitudes every year . . .'

'*Improving the atmosphere of an invalid's room:* Pour some Eau de Cologne onto a shovel, and with a lighted match set fire to it. Move freely around the room. The spirit will make a pretty flame, and impart a delightful refreshing odour to the room . . .'

'*Hiccups, a cure:* Drink half a teaspoonful of vinegar, and keep your arms in an upright position until you feel it necessary to lower them . . .'

'*A cold:* A good remedy for a cold is to spread a piece of brown paper with pig's lard, then sprinkle over sulphur, and wear it next to the chest . . .'

SUPER
SILK UNDIES

A WOMAN'S WORK-LOAD is now lighter than ever before, with the help of hi-tech gadgets, so there is perhaps a greater need to express ourselves creatively and individually. The very womanly art of needlework fulfills this perfectly for me. It is not simply a relaxing pastime, but a solace, a joy and a constant creative challenge. It is exacting work fashioning something beautiful with your own hands, but it is also very satisfying. I am a self-confessed amateur, but I could not resist an attempt to make myself some ritzy, exquisite silk undies. They are the epitome of feminine luxury, and normally beyond the price-range of most of us. You can save pounds by making them yourself, so I found it quite a challenge.

It was an ambitious project, but I was pleased to discover how comparatively simple it turned out to be. And it was a sheer delight to work with pure silk satin. I knew exactly the fabric and colour I wanted, and headed for the sales. Sadly, when I got there the silk had not been reduced, and there were no suitable remnants, but I was so psyched-up for the project that I splashed out and bought it off the roll. Next time I will scour all the sales until I find the right bargain.

A set of underwear could, of course, be made for a third of the cost in man-made fibre. But let's be honest, a chain-store polyester petticoat doesn't have quite the same aura of excitement as the real thing in sensuous silk.

I went to Liberty, in London, as much for the peace and quiet as the wide selection of fabrics. And the tea-room is decorated in Liberty prints and softly lit: the perfect place for quiet reflection on needlework shopping expeditions. I met an old lady who told me that she used to make lingerie for the toffs, and that the lace should ideally be in pure silk too, to avoid washing problems. However, it seems rather elusive these days. I certainly couldn't find any, but I was reassured that pure cotton lace would do almost as well.

I wanted to make the slip in a larger size, because I do not think they should hug the figure and fit exactly. Silk should caress the body in soft folds, and cutting on the cross helps the fabric to hang beautifully. The shop assistant told me that you should allow a smidgeon for shrinkage, and that the high gloss of the silk satin would tone down a little with washing. I also invested in a bottle of special liquid soap for silks, which I will wash by hand, spin gently and iron on the wrong side to protect the gloss.

Although I had many finishing ideas of my own, I opted for a pattern to cut out the basic petticoat and French knickers. The silk satin came in various colours and this time I chose oyster – perhaps, next time, black!

First, however, I had to make sure that I could buy the right coloured lace to match the fabric.

As I planned to hand-stitch, I bought two spools of lovely pure silk thread to work with. The pattern required 1.60 m (5 ft), at 1.15 m (3 ft 6 in) wide, for the slip and 1 m (3 ft) the same width for the knickers. Actually, I found that after cutting out the slip I had enough left over for the knickers. So I managed to get both from 1.60 m (5 ft), which brought down the price considerably and left me with a piece of beautiful silk to spare. I toyed with the idea of making a half-slip, or an envelope to keep my undies in, and the envelope won. Now, with all the right underwear, I'm just waiting for an invitation to travel on the Orient Express!

Later, feeling quite inspired, I designed and made some French knickers in cotton. They can be made in any fabric, and are quite quick and easy to put together. If you decide to have a try, don't worry if you encounter a shortage of attractive lace, because there are other ways of trimming and finishing which are equally pretty.

GENERAL HINTS ON WORKING WITH SILK

The first lesson I learned with silk undies is to use the shortest and finest needle you can cope with practically. Because of my poor eyesight I found it took longer to thread, but I ensured, as always, that I worked in a good light, and used the magnifying glass I hang round my neck. It is important, too, to keep your work in a bag to prevent it looking crumpled before it is even finished.

If you decide to buy a pattern, it may assume, as mine did, that you are more experienced than you really are, so I readily pass on a few tips which I found helpful. I firstly ironed out the pattern, and carefully pressed the silk satin on the wrong side (I do wish I hadn't let the boys use my scissors to cut out cardboard, though!). As the silk is very slippy,

Opposite *As silk underwear is so expensive to buy, I decided to have a go at making my own. I made this petticoat and French knickers out of oyster-coloured silk, and trimmed both with cotton lace in the same colour.*

I pinned down the centre of the pattern to hold it in position before pinning the sides. Do use brass-plated pins whenever possible. Ask for the very fine ones for delicate fabrics, not the coarser type for lace. They have the added bonus of being longer, and do not mark the silk, as steel often does. Do not pin your pattern at the very edge, but a little way in. You can avoid any waste by laying out all the pattern pieces on the fabric before cutting it out. I had great satisfaction in cutting so economically, it was worth the extra few minutes arranging the pattern. It is essential to have no distractions, and it is a good idea to study the pattern in detail before starting.

If you use a thimble, make sure it is a smooth one. Don't experiment in any way on the fabric you have cut – try ideas out on a scrap first. Delicate handling and beautiful stitching are all part of the joy of making-up exquisite lingerie. Lead pencils tend to soil and smudge; on silk satin a thumb-nail is quite effective for marking out the fabric.

I found it better to complete each section of the pattern as far as possible before assembling the whole thing. I was pleasantly surprised to find that silk satin was easier to manipulate and stitch than I had anticipated. I am not sure what it would be like to machine-sew, but hand-stitching gives a certain elasticity and is easier to handle. The rouleaux bands, incidentally, were a piece of cake because the fabric was so slippy. They simply glided the right way out when I pulled them through.

FRENCH KNICKERS

French knickers are lovely to wear in summer, refreshingly cool, as well as flattering to the thighs! I love them because they look so feminine and pretty, and they are also heaven for anyone who suffers from thrush or irritation, which can be exacerbated by tight nylon underwear.

Once I had made the silk underwear from a basic pattern, I had the confidence to plunge in and try some more in cotton, using my own design and variations. It was surprisingly simple.

The knickers can be made very cheaply from fine lawn, which is widely available from department stores and fabric shops. You could be adventurous and use silk. As the amount of fabric needed is so small it is really a good idea to look around for remnants.

I used approximately 85 sq cm (1 sq yd) of fabric and folded it diagonally. The knickers are cut on the cross like the slip and, of course, hang so much better for it.

Firstly, however, it is important to make a paper pattern. Mine is for 86–91 cm (34–36 in) hips, and allows for tiny seams and hems. The back and front are almost identical, except for the gussets – the back gusset is cut 5 cm (2 in) longer than the front.

A Stitch in Time

Obviously not everyone is the same size, and although the measurements given are for 86–91 cm (34–36 in) hips it is easy to adjust them for a larger size. For 96 cm (38 in) hips add 12 mm ($\frac{1}{2}$ in) to the side seam of the front and back pattern pieces and increase the depth by approximately 2.5 cm (1 in).

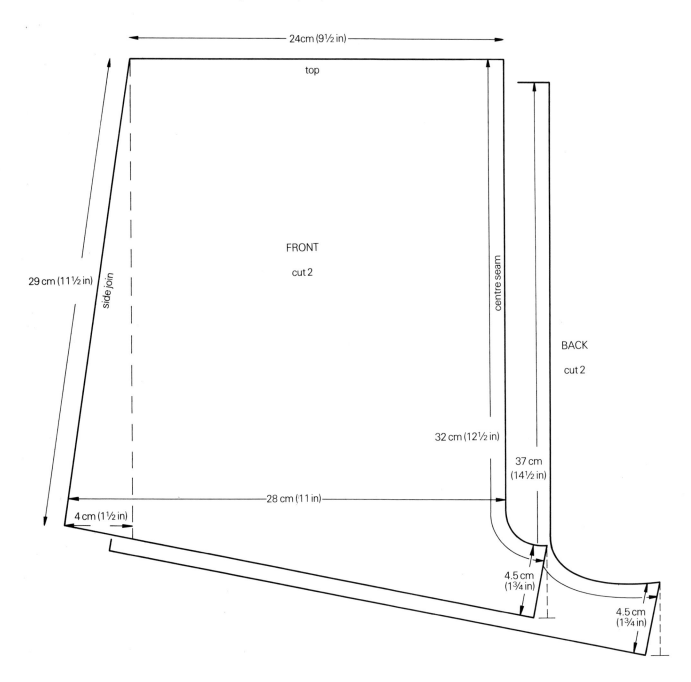

As you can see, the side seam of the paper pattern is not cut straight but is flared, and the bottom hem slopes up towards the sides. When cutting the centre seam, cut from the top straight down for about 28 cm (11 in) before curving outwards for the gusset. The seam underneath the gusset curve is also cut away on a slant to prevent bulkiness between the legs.

One thing I should mention is that French knickers look much larger than conventional ones. They don't stretch, and shouldn't fit exactly but just fall in delicate folds. So if you think yours are looking too baggy do try them on before you make adjustments. I had an anxious moment, but found they were exactly right when I'd finished the elastic.

Cutting out

Make sure the piece of fabric is square, and then fold it diagonally. Lay your paper pattern on the fabric so that the side seams of the pattern pieces lie along the folded edge (see page 90).

Now pin your pattern to the fabric, and when you are satisfied cut it out. If you feel unsure of the tiny hems, allow yourself approximately 5 mm ($\frac{1}{4}$ in) all round. Don't worry – they won't look enormous when they're on!

Before removing the paper pattern, cut the folded edge of the fabric along the side seams.

Don't throw even the smallest scrap of silk away! They are handy for trimmings or appliqué; there may even be enough to make a small brooch cushion for your dressing table.

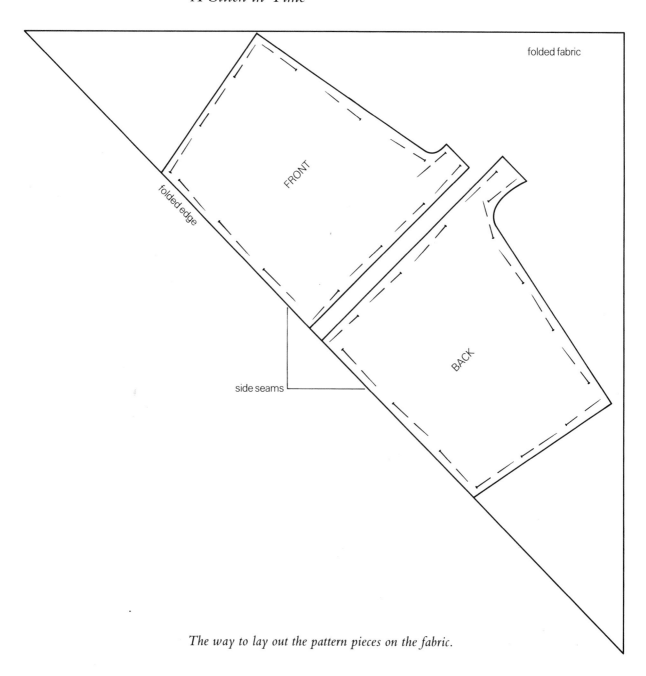

folded fabric

folded edge

FRONT

BACK

side seams

The way to lay out the pattern pieces on the fabric.

Example of gusset curve.

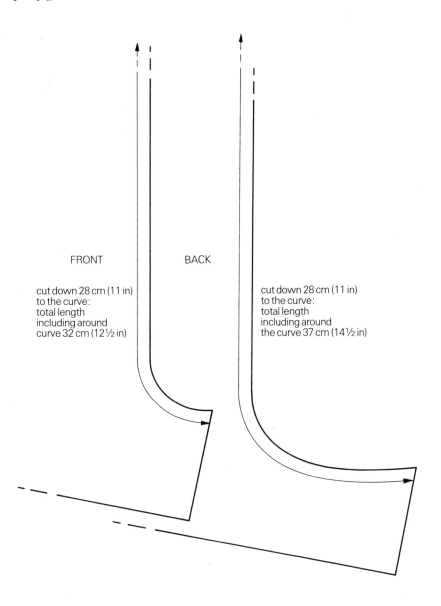

FRONT

BACK

cut down 28 cm (11 in)
to the curve:
total length
including around
curve 32 cm (12½ in)

cut down 28 cm (11 in)
to the curve:
total length
including around
the curve 37 cm (14½ in)

If you decide to curve the sides of your knickers, now is the time to trim your fabric. Shell edging is almost as simple as plain hemming, and is beautifully effective. Lace, faggoting and binding are, of course, suitable alternatives for curved edges. Make a gentle curve in pencil on both the front and back of your pattern pieces, and check they are identical before you actually cut the fabric. Perhaps the best way is to pin the front and back pieces together and cut the curve through all four layers of fabric.

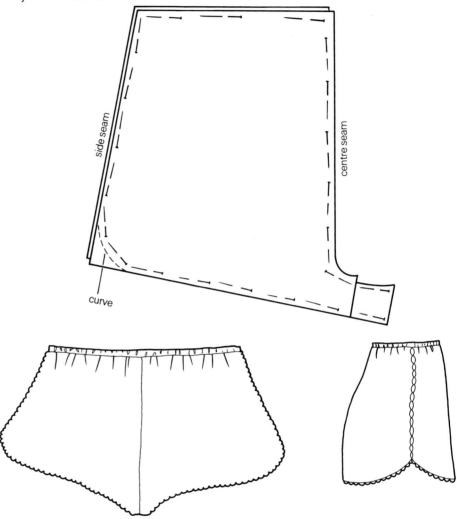

Joining the centre seams

Place the right sides of the two front pieces together, pin down the centre seam and along the gusset curve. Tack, and then either machine-sew or hand-stitch. Repeat for the back.

With such delicate items the finish is important. Try to make neat, flat seams that are as unobtrusive as possible. I treat each seam as if it was a work of art. As they are so small, you don't have the feeling that you'll never finish. You can afford to take time and pride in your work.

I finished off my seams by oversewing in buttonhole stitch. You can, however, roll in the raw edge and sew it along the original stitch line using tiny hem stitches.

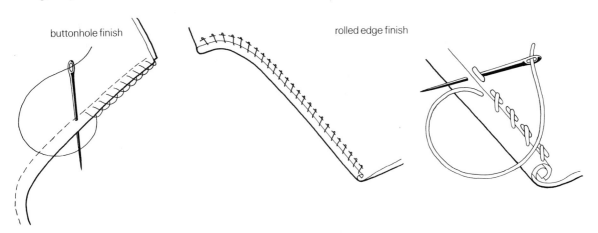

When you have finished, press each seam lightly, open them out and press again.

Joining the front and back
Place right sides together. Keeping the front and back opened out, pin and tack the gusset seam; then sew and finish off as neatly as before. Once again, press lightly when you have finished.

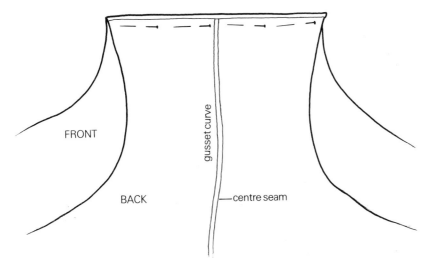

Trimmings
The next step depends on which trimming you have decided to use. Binding or lace can be added now by opening out the knickers and

pinning it from the curve at the leg opening and up to the opposite curve (as shown on the diagram). Then repeat on the other side. If you are using lace, after stitching, oversew the raw edge of the satin lying underneath the lace.

Shell edging and faggoting can be worked right down the four side seams and around the leg openings. Then, when assembling the sides, join the faggoted edge with twisted insertion stitch, and the shell edging with invisible stitches on the wrong side. The result is a pretty peephole effect. Details of both these finishes are given at the end of this section.

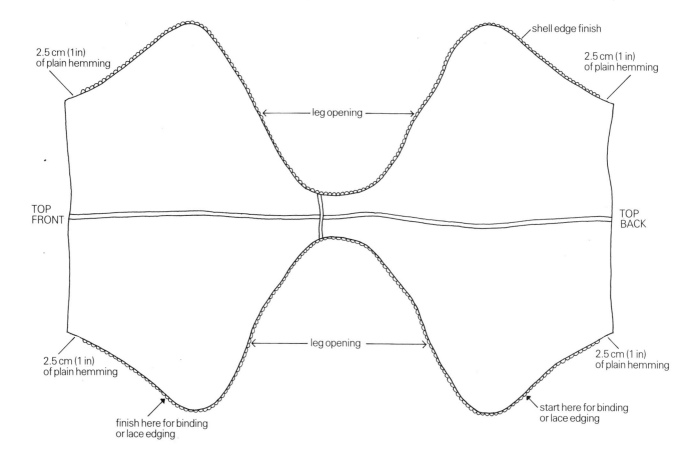

The gusset lining

The gusset lining can be cut from a scrap of cotton lawn, or knitted cotton.

The line A/B (approximately one-third of the way along the gusset lining) indicates where the gusset lies on the seam that joins the front to the back of the knickers.

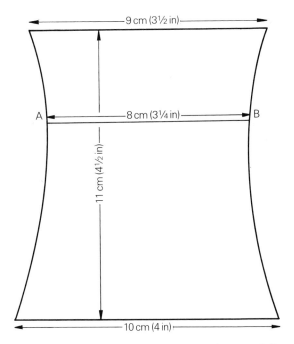

Open out the knickers and pin on the gusset lining. I found it best to pin across the gusset seam with one or two pins before smoothing out and turning in the raw edges.

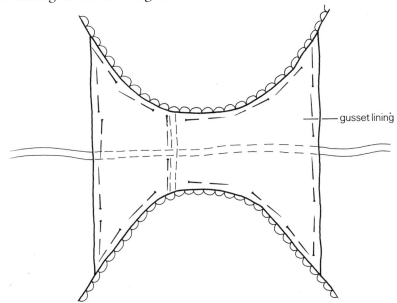

gusset lining

Do take time to manoeuvre the lining and if necessary trim it a little. Tack round it, and then make absolutely sure the lining fits snugly before stitching around by hand.

Joining the side seams

Working on the wrong side, pin and tack the front side seam to the back side seam on both sides. You can machine-sew or hand-stitch the side seams, finishing off as before.

To join shell edging, match up the shells and sew by hand with tiny firm stitches so that you create a peep-hole effect. The first 2.5 cm (1 in), however, must be sewn straight to accommodate a hem for the elastic at the top of the knickers.

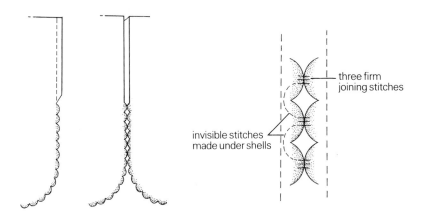

The elasticated waist

Turn over a folded hem, no more than 12 mm ($\frac{1}{2}$ in) deep. Machine or run stitch around, remembering to leave a small gap to thread the elastic through.

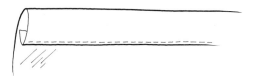

Make another row of stitching fractionally down from the top for a neat finish.

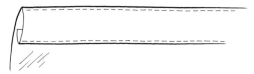

Measure around your waist to find how much elastic you need, add a little to join, and thread it through with a safety pin. Sew the elastic ends together by placing one on top of the other, and stitch up the gap in the hem. *C'est fini!*

Some variations:

A faggoted finish.

Brief with a soft lace trim. The
sides are much shorter, but
the back is usually a little
more full than the front
in this style.

An appliqué finish.

SLIP WITH FAGGOTING DETAIL

If you adapt a pattern and add faggoting, remember to buy more fabric than stated, but there is no need to buy lace as well.

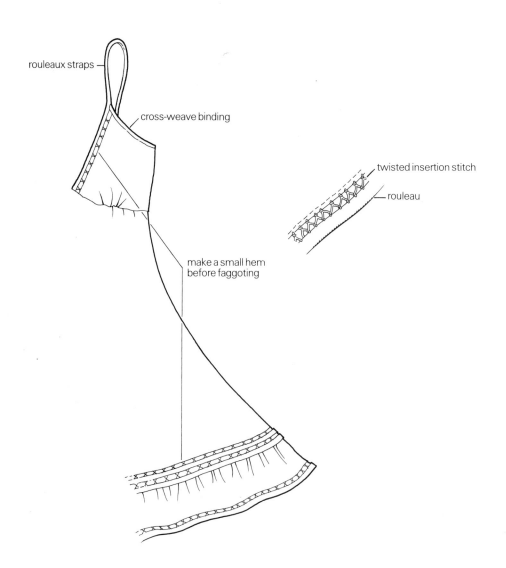

rouleaux straps

cross-weave binding

twisted insertion stitch

rouleau

make a small hem before faggoting

To make the rouleaux
Fold the fabric across a square and measure the diagonal length. This is the length of your rouleau. If it is not long enough, either fold a larger square or cut two or more strips and join them. For more rouleaux, continue to cut strips from the diagonal edge. The strips should be about 2.5–4 cm (1–1½ in) wide.

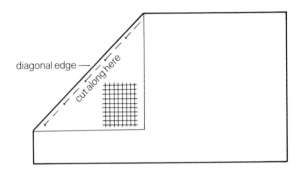

Fold the strip and run stitch along the raw edges.

Slip the rouleaux needle inside and tack stitch it to one end. Rouche up the fabric and pull the needle through.

Finally, press flat along the seam.

Faggoting

If you are adapting a pattern for faggoting, cut back the fabric edge by about 6 mm ($\frac{1}{4}$ in) and make a tiny folded hem along the raw edge. In this way, you will lose just over 12 mm ($\frac{1}{2}$ in), which is taken up by the faggoting.

Pin the hemmed fabric onto strong brown paper and, leaving a gap of 6 mm ($\frac{1}{4}$ in), pin the rouleau alongside it. Tack into position and work along in twisted insertion stitch, picking up only the fabric and not the brown paper.

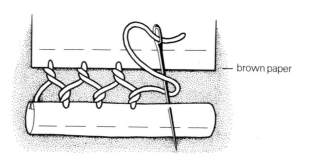

A small stitch is taken alternately on each piece of fabric to be joined. The needle always enters the fabric from beneath and is twisted once round the thread before making the next stitch, on the opposite piece of fabric.

Joining a frill to a rouleau

Cut a cross-weave strip for the rouleau but do not sew it up. Gather up the frill and with right sides facing, pin it along the rouleau strip. Tack and then stitch along with running stitch or by machine.

Gently press open the seam. Make a small turn-in at the top of the rouleau and fold it completely in half. Pin into place along the stitch line and hemstitch down on the wrong side. The frilled rouleau can now be joined with twisted insertion stitch.

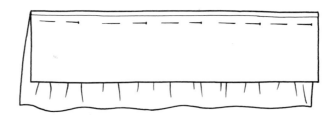

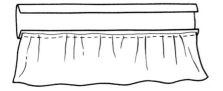
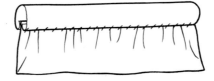

Some useful stitches

Hemstitching

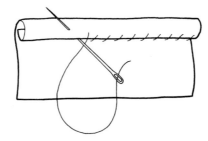

Shell edging

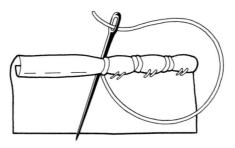

The shell edging is formed simultaneously with the hemstitching, on the wrong side. Fold and tack a narrow hem, then work a double overcast stitch, followed by one or two tiny hemstitches on the wrong side. Repeat the overcast stitches at even intervals of approximately 6mm ($\frac{1}{4}$ in) and keep the hemstitches as invisible as possible.

Eyelets
The embroidery on lingerie should be worked to enhance the beauty of the fabric. It should therefore be simple and fairly plain.

Repetition of a simple shape, such as tiny eyelets, works well.

Work a small circle of running stitch and then pierce the centre with a stiletto.

Opposite *I made a silk envelope from leftover scraps of material to keep my new undies in. It is an ideal way of packing them for travelling as it prevents them from getting creased.*

Tuck the raw edge under as you oversew closely around the hole. If you are working on silk use a pure silk thread.

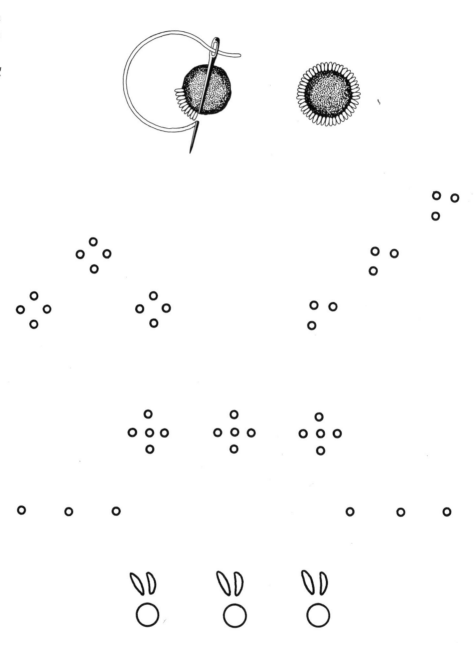

SILK ENVELOPE

I decided to make a silk envelope to protect my new undies. I got the inspiration from a kimono my sister brought back for me from the Far East. It was beautifully presented in its own silk sachet. It really is a good idea, because once you've put your undies in the envelope, they're not slipping all over the drawer and getting creased and crinkled. It's also the most efficient way of packing them for travelling.

Silk satin has a soft crêpe underside, which I used for contrasting bands and piping to decorate the envelope. Next to the bands, I used a strip of lace, which I carefully cut into narrower lengths. The lace was actually very versatile. Although I bought just one width, I found I could cut it into narrower strips and also snip out little motifs and flowers.

To fasten my envelope I chose a natural mother-of-pearl button from my collection. It's not too heavy and has a beautiful lustre which compliments the silk satin.

The most delightful thing about the envelope is that it was made entirely from scraps, which left me with a feeling of almost smug satisfaction.

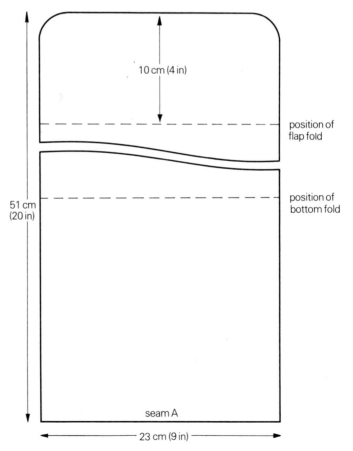

When the envelope is made up it measures approximately 20 × 23 cm (8 × 9 in). Even though it is a simple shape to cut out, it is advisable to make a paper pattern first.

I had sufficient silk satin left to cut out a single piece of fabric for the envelope. I used the same pattern to cut out the lining from a pale flesh-coloured scrap of silk.

The trimmings are added before the envelope is made up.

Trimming

Using my silk satin scraps, I managed to cut a narrow strip on the cross-weave which I used crêpe-side-out as piping. Without joins you will need a strip about 40 cm (16 in) long. The crêpe bands are just 23 cm (9 in) long and about 2 cm ($\frac{3}{4}$ in) wide before turnings.

It is not necessary to pipe seam A, but if you have enough fabric it makes a nice finishing touch. Again cutting on the cross-weave and using it crêpe-side-out, you would need a 23 cm (9 in) strip.

Taking into account the markings for the flap fold, pin on the crêpe bands and lace and, when you are happy with their position, neatly hemstitch.

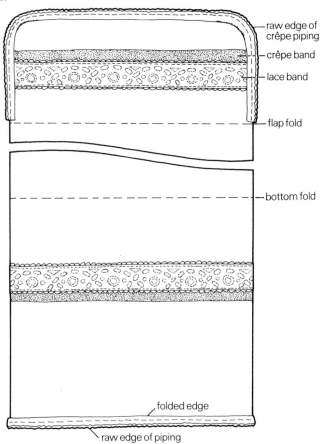

Next, pin and tack on the piping. Mine is very narrow and I didn't bother with piping cord.

The button-loop
This is made from a short length of rouleau, a piece left over from the piping should do. Fold it lengthways and run stitch along before turning right-side out with a rouleau needle. When you have pinned it into position and checked that it fits over your button, run stitch around the piping to hold it firmly. Remove all the pins and tacking and press lightly on the wrong side.

The lining
To join the lining, place right sides of the two pieces of fabric together and pin around, leaving seam A open for turning right-side-out. Work a tiny running stitch or backstitch around and trim off any excess edging. Turn right-side-out and pin and tack seam A, which should be finished in a tiny hemstitch picking up the original seam on the piping.

Finishing
Gently press on the wrong side and fold seam A up to the flap fold so the envelope is inside out. Join the side seams making a few extra stitches at the openings. Turn the whole bag right-side-out and add the button.
   Voila!

COLLECTABLES

I'M SOMETHING of a magpie when it comes to collecting things for my home. I like to buy knives, forks and china which is neither in, nor out, of fashion. Beautiful tableware somehow seems to make the meal taste better. I try to buy the best I can afford at the time, but I usually wait until I have the money if it is quite expensive. In the end I do believe it works out more economically as I am not continually buying things to make do for a while. And if I crack a lovely dish, I don't worry too much, because it still looks and feels nice.

Things don't have to be perfect to be worth keeping if you are fond of them. The candlestick is cracked, the mug is chipped, and the clock doesn't work, but they still look nice with the other things on my kitchen shelf.

Collecting is great fun – I have amassed bottles, pots, ribbons, scraps of lace and pieces of glassware to keep for my grandchildren. Even a pair of clumpy 1960s block shoes with 20 cm (8 in) platforms have gone into the attic. In years to come they'll hoot over them. It is an absorbing hobby which I indulge as I travel round the country. I have also kept all the different spectacles I have worn over the years, and some of the early ones are quite funny now. Experience has taught me that the only way to prevent my collections from taking the house over, is to keep them beautifully tidy. Pretty boxes with lids, and baskets, are perfect for storage; they stop things spilling over into drawers and filling up cupboards. A good, old-fashioned, treasure chest, big enough to hold lots of things, is ideal for the attic.

I try to keep a box full of cards suitable for birthdays and thank-you's. Some are really-bad-taste examples from the 1960s, with hipsters and big hats. It has become quite a competition among my friends to see who can find the worst cards (you get the best in Spain). Cards are inexpensive to collect, and it is surprising how many you can find in the January sales and in sundry countries.

Jumble sales can be very rewarding, though I do not get the opportunity to visit as many as I would like. I have picked up some lovely old buttons and unusual fabrics in charity shops. A friend of mine goes to look for cotton pieces which she uses for her patchwork. Another collects unusually-patterned fabrics, such as moss crêpe and crêpe-de-Chine. I remember my mother used to buy woollen jumpers and, if they were in good condition, she would unravel them and wind them into a hank. If you wash the bank and hang it on the line with a weight on the end, it takes out all the crinkles, and you can knit it up like new. If the wool is not a particularly nice colour, you can knit it double with a complimentary colour to give a tweed effect.

One of my greatest finds was a pair of men's cream linen trousers in an Oxfam shop. They were beautiful quality, and had never been worn. Even the original labels and tags were still on. I paid £3 for them, took them home, and altered and re-pleated them. Later I was delighted to see a pair of almost identical heavy linen trousers in Ralph Lauren for more than £100.

I collect all kinds of needlework by artists whose stitchcraft I admire. They range from unknown Victorians to contemporary needle-women, and I use some pieces to learn new stitches and methods.

I recently commissioned a needlepoint picture, taken from a photograph of myself and the boys on our favourite beach in Greece. I met Linda McDevitt, who made it, at a needlework exhibition which I had been asked to help judge. I asked her to leave the faces on her needlepoint picture blank, but to make them easily recognizable from their shape and hair outline. If you enjoy needlepoint it might be fun to try copying a family picture. Linda's work, now framed, looks beautiful in my sitting room.

I want to be an old lady surrounded by memories and reminders of the past, and have lots of heirlooms and photographs to pass down the family. As well as buying commemorative ware for the home, and signing and dating all my needlework, I try to keep other records of family life. We live in such a throw-away age that treasured mementoes so easily vanish for ever if we do not make the effort to keep them for future generations. I sometimes regret all the photographs which were never taken – monthly profiles of me, for instance, when I was pregnant, and before-and-after pictures when moving to a new house.

All the cars we own in the course of a lifetime are worth recording, too. My grandchildren may never see a Mini, or if they do it may be in a museum. It would be nice to buy a miniature model each time you change your car; one of those Matchbox or Dinky things. My friend Lorraine Chase has a beautifully restored Georgian house, and on the shelf she keeps a pair of those wonderfully stylish stilettoes we all used to have, alongside a remarkable pair of two-tone platform shoes. They are a delightful touch of eccentricity, as well as of historic interest. History, after all, is today's news tomorrow.

I have decided this year to keep an album on the piano next to a little basket of scissors, glue and sticky tape. I have started to keep a record of headlines which catch my eye, plus things like coins and bank notes that go out of circulation, and lots of family photographs. The boys are helping me, and we are including their best drawings and stories. If we go to the theatre, or visit a museum, the tickets and programmes will be stuck in too. Hopefully it will blossom into a diary of the whole family,

Above *These needlepoint pictures are very special records of life with my family, on holiday and at home.*
Left *Linda McDevitt, who made the pictures, copied this one from a photograph of myself and the boys on our favourite beach in Greece.* Right *The Stubbs family at home. I asked Linda to leave our faces blank, but to make us easily recognizable from our shape and hair outline. That's me, next to Jason – the tall one!*

Opposite *Many of my collections are personal mementoes, such as this basket full of all the different spectacles I have worn over the years.*

Right *I have a large collection of needlework which includes some beautifully embroidered pictures such as this one.*

a record of both current affairs and the little things which touched us personally. I looked at scrap books in the stationers', but decided against them because they looked so naff. The biggest problem was finding one with a cover which would endure the years, and have plenty of room inside to stick in things like a lock of hair from when the children were blonde, or a baby tooth.

*   *   *

CHRISTMAS AGAIN

I'M SURE most women inwardly groan when Christmas comes around. After all the preparations, shopping, cooking and generally getting the house ready, all I want to do are the things that mums are not supposed to do – like flopping in the chair all day watching television. Everyone becomes so harrassed instead of doing the sensible thing and getting a little tipsy, relaxing and really enjoying everything.

Christmas lunch has taken upon itself an importance out of all proportion. I sometimes think that the hysteria and panic about getting the turkey right, and serving up enormous mounds of food for everyone becomes slightly ridiculous. I would much sooner join in the fun, watch the children open their presents, and spend time with my family and friends than retreat to the kitchen. Why not dig in your heels and take the time to do your hair, put on some make-up and look a little ritzy on Christmas Day. I'm sure the family would prefer a pretty, fluffy mum to share the enjoyment with them, not the snappy figure pushing her hair out of her eyes with an oven glove, bawling at them to tidy up the wrapping paper, 'And for goodness sake will *someone* set the table!'

It is nice to keep Christmas traditional with a cake and pudding, a tree, decorations, cards and gifts, but it's no fun propping yourself against the kitchen door as if you have been buried alive for three days.

I used to dread going to other people's homes because of the silent hysteria over food. I recall going to a friend's house, and they had invited a very famous Italian guest and – of all things – they had decided to cook an Italian meal. The whole time you could hear utter panic ricochetting round the kitchen because it hadn't turned out right. For goodness sake, I thought, why didn't you give him fish and chips – at least he wouldn't have known if it was right or not.

Mince pies and cakes and puddings are fine because they can all be done before the day. The Big Dinner has become an anachronism, left over from upstairs-downstairs days. It is hard work for a woman to cope single-handed with a huge meal with all the trimmings. It is no surprise that millions feel resentful and martyred because they have missed out on the morning's fun. Enlisting help doesn't make things better – roping-in grandma and grandpa to tackle the mountain of dishes rather puts the damper on their spirits too. People like visiting each other on Christmas Day for the family company and conversation; they don't really want to see a *prima donna* performance over what, after all, is just one more meal to add to the hundreds you have cooked all year round.

You could keep it very simple with some lovely smoked salmon, or baked potatoes; or produce something rich like eggs benedict. And if Aunty Maud starts tutting and clicking because it wasn't traditional don't worry, you might win her round one day. If the atmosphere was warm and friendly and everyone had a whale-up because of it, then it was worth it. If more women explained that they are inviting everyone for Christmas, but this year it is going to be different, it would work because nobody wants to be on their own. It is really the children and the company they look forward too.

Christmas preparations needn't be a problem. I go to bed with the Christmas cake recipe book and study it so that I know it pretty thoroughly. I even write it down if necessary, then I say to the family: 'Right, Friday night's Christmas cake night, let's all make it.' And next week, the same with the pudding. You could make a party of it by inviting friends round. Make a mound of sandwiches and lay on lashings of lemonade and Guinness. Then, if you want to get pleasantly tiddled, you can. After all, no one deserves it more.

I used to let the boys decorate the Christmas tree, but somehow it always ended up looking like a drag queen standing in the corner, tilted and slightly tipsy. As I am going through a stylish, silvery-white phase at the moment, I do the tree myself when they are not there. I'll say: 'You don't mind, do you? It's not very boyish. Leave it to me and I'll just keep it very simple.' I quietly handed all the old baubles their notice and used them for decorating Christmas gifts. I decked the tree completely in white with twinkly mirrors on long strings, instead of tarnished tinsel.

If you are having a pre-Christmas clear-out, please don't forget the teenagers. Children's homes often get lots of toys, but seldom anything suitable for older children. I try to pack up all those lipsticks and nail varnishes and eye-shadow I never got around to using in a pretty make-

up purse, along with bubble bath and toilet water that I haven't opened. There are lots of other things, such as tights and gloves, which perhaps you haven't worn or don't need, which are really welcomed.

If your children are anything like mine, they must get terribly curious about Christmas presents. They usually shake and rattle them, and smooth down the wrapping paper to read through it, and know almost exactly what each one contains. Last year I spent a whole afternoon determined to foil them. When the boys smoothed down the paper they read horrifying labels such as Cindy Doll, or Fairies' Home. I had cut advertisements from magazines and stuck them underneath the wrapping. Then I disguised the shapes by taping on toilet rolls, and anything which made strange sounds, like packets of seeds and boxes of nails.

Selecting presents for the family is fun, but for friends it can be a problem – so many different things, and so little time to choose.

Last year I decided to choose the same gift for everyone, and settled on a beautiful book called *French Style*. This year I have already found a potter who makes beautiful mugs, so I am buying two each for everyone I know, and Christmas will be taken care of. The trick is to get something that everyone is sure to like.

All year round I collect boxes, which I put aside for packing and wrapping gifts. I choose paper, usually from the January sales, which is suitable for any kind of gift. It works out cheaper to buy it in a roll, because you don't have to struggle to join sheets, and a lot of wastage is saved on smaller presents.

If you are not very good with ribbons and bows, try this simple wrapping method, which looks particularly good on men's gifts. Cut your paper to size, and add at least 8–9 cm (3–3½ in) on one side.

Fold the extra strip of paper over:

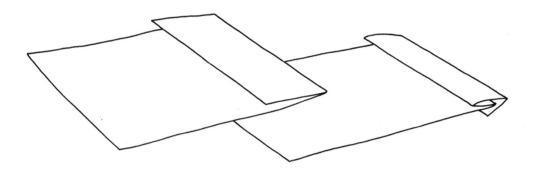

Now fold it back again, to form a band:

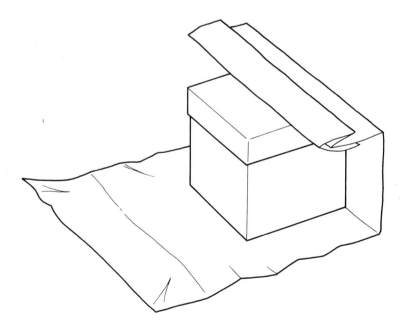

Wrap the paper around the gift so that the band is uppermost:

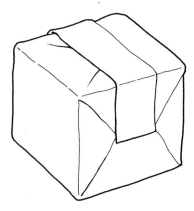

Turn and fold in the corners neatly, and stick down each side. Slip your card inside the fold on the front.

Throughout the year I try to give gifts which I would like to receive myself – things which last and are worthy of a place in any home. I like to give commemorative china, which I usually buy in threes, anyway, for my sons; like those funny mugs which stand on big feet, or that wonderful Prince Charles mug with the big ears which I am still cursing I didn't get for myself. Presents needn't be expensive. I have a small Charles and Diana wedding-picture tin, which I use for my buttons. It is a little worn and scratched now and beginning to look suitably collectable. Commemorative tins are reasonably priced, available everywhere, and it is nice to fill them with sweets or biscuits.

And that relative who is always in the dog-house for forgetting birthdays: don't just buy him a diary or calendar, fill in all the anniversaries and school holidays too. Everyone loses small pencil sharpeners, and an office desk-model is always useful for someone to put on a shelf at home.

A lovely summer gift is to wash some strawberries, dry them well, leaving on the little green stalk, and dip the tips into melted chocolate. Leave them to dry on non-stick baking parchment, and arrange them in a pretty bowl, or even back in a newly-lined punnet. The green stalks, red berries and brown chocolate look delicious and are lovely served with coffee.

If friends are stuck for cash, I like to buy silly things I wouldn't normally give. I fill a big basket with all the items they will be cutting down on, like cigarettes, a bottle of wine and packets of J-cloths, and add a bottle of perfume as a morale-booster.

Friends who live in the country love to receive anything with Harrods' name on, like a pot of cheese or a cream jug. They are also appreciated because they become collector's items. Harrods occasionally do unique lines which they don't seem to repeat, such as little tins of sweets in the shape of a Harrods van with wheels on. Liberty's and Fortnum's gifts go down equally well, especially if they are packaged so that the containers can be collected afterwards.

Most people have plants which look lovely in terracotta pots and saucers. The big ones look beautiful standing on the floor, and the little ones, of course, are less expensive and look good anywhere. I also like buying clusters of candles in all shapes and sizes – those fat ones which don't need a holder with, say, a long tall one, a short fat one and a tiny one to go with them.

People used to groan at the thought of receiving handkerchiefs, but today, when there are so many allergies, tissues are not as popular as they were. My family have gone off them, and if you have hay fever it is wise to avoid them because of the particles of dust they exude. A little basket, or box, of handkerchiefs may once again be recognized as an attractive, useful gift.

As children seem to get masses of felt-tip pens, which come in a whole range of colours, I think a set of really good paint brushes and water colours makes a change for them.

A pretty gift for a little girl – or even a big one for that matter – is a basket filled with rolls of satin ribbons in various shades, along with some of those gimmicky little bobbles, hair-slides and combs.

When a friend has a baby, I usually choose something dark for them. I suppose it may be because when I was young, during World War II, I had to wear skirts made out of black-out material with yards and yards

of coloured binding sewn on around the bottom to brighten them up. I do like dark colours on babies because it compliments their rosy cheeks. A friend bought some navy dungarees in the crawling size, and I loved them. They were quite large and I used to put them on baby with giant-sized turn-ups. A pair of those baby Kickers look so sweet on the nursery shelf, waiting to be worn. And there are some wonderful humorous outfits around, like T-shirts with 'IT WALKS' printed on them. Or you could get something plain and embroider on it yourself. I used to enjoy receiving those gifts because I found I had an overload of pastel knitted clothes.

Over the years I have received some marvellous gifts – funny ones, hand-made ones, and some very expensive ones. But this year I was secretly very disappointed that no one thought to buy me Arthur Marshall. I hinted enough . . . ah well, maybe next year.

A YEAR GOES EVER SO QUICK

Did you keep to all your plans this
year? No, I didn't either . . . but I'll
do it next year.